Reading in Content Areas

STRATEGIES FOR READING SUCCESS

Level B

Program Consultant
Dr. Kate Kinsella

San Francisco State University
San Francisco, California

Upper Saddle River, New Jersey
www.globefearon.com

Consultants

John Edwin Cowen, Ed.D.
Assistant Professor, Education/Reading;
Program Coordinator, Graduate M.A.T./
Elementary Education
School of Education
Fairleigh Dickinson University
Teaneck, NJ

Dr. Kate Kinsella
Dept. of Secondary Education and
Step to College Program
San Francisco State University
San Francisco, CA

Reviewers

Bettye J. Birden
Reading Specialist
McReynolds Middle School
Houston, TX

Sally Parker, M.A.
T.R. Smedberg Middle School/
Sheldon High School
Elk Grove, Unified School District
Elk Grove, CA

Georgeanne Herbeck
District Supervisor, Elementary Education
Perth Amboy, NJ

Kenneth J. Ratti
Science Department Chairman
Vaca Peña Middle School
Vacaville, CA

Senior Editor: Lynn W. Kloss
Editor: Monica Glina
Editorial Assistant: Kevin Iwano
Writers: Sandra Widener, Terri Flynn-Nason
Production Editor: Alan Dalgleish
Cover and Interior Design: Lisa Nuland
Electronic Page Production: José López

Photo Credits
p. 6: PhotoDisc, Inc.; **p. 10:** NASA; **p. 14:** National Portrait Gallery, Washington; **p. 26:** Nubar Alexanian;
p. 29: U.S. Army Photograph; **p. 36:** UPI/Corbis-Bettmann; **p. 61:** Archive Photos; **p. 71:** The Granger Collection;
p. 83: NASA; **p. 93:** David Seelig, Allsport; **p. 93:** Jed Jacobsohn, Allsport; **p. 108:** Jim Wilson, NYT Pictures.

Printed in the United States of America   5 6 7 8 9 10   04 03 02 01 00
ISBN: 0-835-95500-1

Globe
Fearon

Contents

To the Student

The Hows and Whys of Reading

Think of a story that you've read. Maybe it was about someone's exciting adventure. What did you want to know about the story? What kinds of questions did you ask to get that information?

If you were reading an adventure story, you probably wanted to know *who* the characters were and *when* and *where* they were going. These questions are very helpful when reading *literary text*, which includes things like short stories, novels, plays, and myths. They all tell a story.

There is another kind of writing that is called *informational text*. This kind of writing informs the reader by giving opinions, explanations, reasons, facts, and examples about a certain topic. Things like chapters in a textbook and newspaper articles are considered informational text, so you are already familiar with this type of writing.

Good Questions for Literary Text	Good Questions for Informational Text
who when where	how what why

Think back to an example of literary text you've read. How are the questions you ask about a story different from the ones you ask when you read a chapter in your science book? In a science book, the questions *how*, *what*, and *why* are a great way to ask the "big" questions and get the information you are looking for. You might even start by changing the bold type headings and topic sentences into questions that begin with *how*, *what*, and *why*. Since *who*, *where* and *when* can be answered with a simple fact or one-word answer, they are not as useful when reading informational text. Look at the following example:

Heading		Question
Promoting Economic Growth	becomes	How can you promote economic growth?
Causes of Earthquakes	becomes	What causes earthquakes?
The Protests Affect U.S. Policy	becomes	Why do the protests affect U.S. policy?

These are examples of "big" questions. It is by asking these big questions that you will get the most out of the informational texts that you read. In this book, you'll learn more strategies for reading informational text and for remembering what you read.

Unit 1
Using Reading Strategies

You probably already use a strategy when you read. Think about what you do when you pick up a magazine. First, you look at the cover. A photograph or headline might catch your eye. You might see a picture of a movie star you know and look for the story in the table of the contents. If the article sounds interesting, you probably turn to that page. Then you look at the article and the photograph. You read the caption under the photo. If you decide you want to find out more, you read the article. You have just used a reading strategy.

In this book, you will learn reading strategies to help you better understand anything you read. You will be able to connect your reading to what you already know. You also will be able to remember what you read.

Becoming an Active Reader

When you use a reading strategy, you become an active reader. You respond to what you read with questions, ideas, and opinions. You also respond by taking notes on what you read. Finally, you think about what you read. What these steps have in common is that you are involved with what you are reading. You are not just reading words. You are having a conversation with the author.

Steps of the Strategies

Different strategies work well for different kinds of readings. However, all of the strategies in this book have some steps in common. Every strategy has four basic steps. First, you preview what you will be reading. Then you read the selection. Your next step is to take notes about what you read. Finally, you review your reading. Below is a drawing of the steps of the reading strategies.

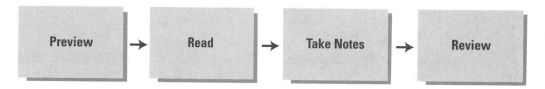

First, preview what you will read. When you begin the reading process, your first step is to think about what you will be reading. You do this by previewing. When you preview, you think about what you already know about the topic. You look for clues about what you might learn. Here are the steps you will use when you preview:

1. Look at the title. What clues does it give you about the topic?

2. Look at the illustrations or diagrams and read the captions. Often, major points are illustrated.

3. Read the first paragraph. It may include a summary of what is to come.

4. Read the last paragraph. It may sum up the writer's main points.

Second, read carefully. As you read, think about what you are reading. What does the author want you to learn? Do you understand all of the words you are reading? Look for the clues that the author has given you.

Third, take notes. The kind of notes you take will vary depending on what you are reading. In math, your notes may be an explanation of how to solve a problem. In social studies, your notes may compare two countries. A researcher found that students remember only 5 to 34 percent of the information they don't take notes on. When you take notes, you put the information in your own words. Notes help the information stay in your mind.

Fourth, review your reading. The kind of review you do depends on the topic and the strategy. You may review a science selection by making a diagram. Often, however, you will write a summary. To write a good summary, you must identify and explain the main points of the reading. Summarizing can help you remember what you have read.

How to Choose a Strategy

A variety of strategies is included in this book because different strategies lend themselves to different types of reading. In addition, people read—and learn—in different ways. After trying each strategy, you may find that one works best for you. Try that strategy with different kinds of reading.

You may also find that one strategy works better on one type of reading than on another. For example, one strategy might work well on an article on how to fix a flat tire. Another strategy might work well on an explanation of a World War II battle.

Experiment with these strategies. You'll find that you can use them on anything you read, both in and out of school. You'll also find that they'll help you make sense of your reading—and remember it!

Strategy 1 PACA

Understand It...... PACA stands for **P**redicting **A**nd **C**onfirming **A**ctivity. Active readers often make a few predictions about an article's topic. While they read, they look for information that will confirm their predictions. The PACA strategy can help make you an active reader, too. It can help you think about what you read.

Try It............... PACA is a good strategy to use when you know something about a topic. You preview the reading, form some ideas about the topic, and make some predictions. Then you read to see whether your predictions are right. If they're wrong, you revise them. You'll probably also find some ideas that you didn't expect.

The article on the next page is about in-line skating. You probably know something about in-line skating. You might have seen people skate. You might have skated yourself. Use what you know to make some predictions about the article. Follow along with a student as he uses the PACA strategy.

Strategy Tip

Base your predictions on *why* you are reading. For example, if you are reading a social studies assignment, your predictions will be different from those you'd make when you are reading a science assignment.

Step 1. Predict what you might learn in the article.

Preview the article to get an idea of what it is about. The student looked at the title, which told him the article was about in-line skating. When he read the subheadings, he knew the article would contain information about safety and basic skills. The student thought about what he already knew about in-line skating. Then he previewed the article. Here is what he thought:

What do I know about in-line skating? I see kids doing it. They seem to really like it. It looks like a cross between ice skating and roller skating. Some skaters go very fast. How do they stay in control?

The student then wrote his predictions in the Predictions column of his PACA chart. Use the PACA chart below to add your own predictions about the article. What other information might the article contain? Use what you know about in-line skating and what you see as you preview the article.

Predictions	Support
the article will talk about the history of in-line skating	
how to skate in races	

Step 2. Read, then confirm your predictions.

First, read the article. Then look at your PACA chart. When you confirm a prediction, make a check mark in the small box next to that prediction. When you find points you did not predict, write them. Then draw a star in the box by each new prediction. If your predictions were wrong, revise them or cross them out. Here's how the student began reading and marking the predictions he made:

Predictions		Support
the article will talk about the history of in-line skating	✓	
~~how to skate in races~~ how to skate safely	★	

In Step With In-Line Skating

In 1760, Joseph Merlin decided to attach wooden spools to the bottoms of his shoes. That way, he thought, he could skate in the summer when there was no ice. Merlin's idea worked fairly well—until he skated into an expensive mirror, shattering it.

The in-line skates of today are much more than wooden spools on a shoe. The in-line skating story of this century began in 1980. That year, two Minnesota brothers tried to figure out a way to practice ice hockey in the summer. They invented the first modern in-line skates.

The idea caught on quickly. By the mid-1990s, in-line skating was *in*. At the start of the 21st century, the sport is still growing. More than six million skaters swoop and glide across paved areas everywhere. If you want to try the sport, however, you need to keep a few things in mind. Think about the equipment you need and about learning to skate safely. Most skaters recommend that you take a couple of lessons before risking your knees—or your neck.

How do you choose skates? The most important factors are the outer boot, the inner boot, and the wheels. The outer boot needs to be stiff enough to support your ankles, especially if you are a beginner. The inner boot should let your foot breathe and feel comfortable. A slight rubbing in the store can mean big blisters on the road.

You'll have to make some decisions about the wheels. First, you need to decide how many wheels you want. Most skates have four wheels. Racing models have five wheels—on those skates, expect to *fly*. Your skates may have only three wheels if you have small feet. The size of the wheels matters too. The smaller the wheel, the slower you will go. Most adults choose wheels from 70 to 72 mm (millimeters) in diameter. Children's wheels may be as small as 64 mm. Racers, who need speed, may go to 80 mm in diameter.

Safety First

Safety is a big issue for in-line skaters. Skaters can move very quickly, and it's easy to wind up on the concrete. No one can promise you won't fall. If you wear the right gear, though, you can avoid serious injury. Along with your skates, you need to buy wrist guards, knee and elbow pads, and a helmet.

The wrist guards help prevent the most common in-line skating injuries: broken and sprained wrists. When you fall, you will probably tumble forward. If you can, get your hands out of the way. However, your instinct will be to try to break your fall with your wrists. Wrist guards can **minimize** an injury. Knee guards and elbow pads provide the same kind of protection for falls involving knees and elbows.

An in-line skater in protective gear soars above a curved ramp.

Wearing a helmet when you skate is as important as wearing a helmet when you ride a bike. Head injuries can be very serious—even fatal. A helmet can prevent or minimize injuries to your head. *Always* wear one. It's that simple.

Blading Basics

The basics of in-line skating are easy to learn. In-line skating is more like ice skating than roller skating. Some people think in-line skating is an easier sport to learn and a lot more fun. When you first try the sport, find a flat, smooth surface such as a parking lot. (Make sure skating is allowed there.) The skating surface should be surrounded by grass, not gravel or dirt. If you need to slow down or can't remember how to stop, you can jump on the grass.

Strategy Tip

When you preview, pay close attention to any photographs you see. What clues does this photograph give you about what might be in the article?

Vocabulary Tip

Even if you don't know the word *minimize,* you may know that the prefix *mini-* means "small." Use that knowledge to help you understand *minimize.*

As in ice skating, you move forward by pushing one foot off to the side. Then you shift your weight to the other leg and push off. Soon you'll find a rhythm, a kind of glide. You also need to learn to stop. Extend your arms for better balance. Push down the heel of your right foot, bending your knees as you do. The brake on your heel will slow you down. Once you're comfortable, you can try fancier ways of stopping.

Consider taking a clinic on blading. Even if you know the basics, you might find an advanced clinic helpful. Learning the tricks of the best skaters can make in-line skating even more fun.

Step 3. Support your predictions with details.

After you finish adding or revising your predictions, look at what you wrote. Each prediction needs details to support it. Write the evidence in the Support column. Here is how the student added to his predictions:

Predictions		Support
the article will talk about the history of in-line skating	✓	first skates in 1760, modern skates in 1980
~~how to skate in races~~ how to skate safely	*	first, find flat pavement or concrete, use side to side gliding motion

Now go back to your predictions. Fill in details in the Support column that will help you remember the main points of the article. When you're finished, keep your PACA chart. You can use it to help you review for a test.

Apply It . . . . Try the PACA strategy with a reading assignment you have. First, preview the assignment and write some predictions about it on a PACA chart. Next, read the assignment. After you read, look for information about the predictions you made. When you find them, add check marks to the small box. When you see points you did not predict, add them to your chart and add stars in the small box. Finally, go back and write the evidence or examples that support each prediction. Your notes should be a good review of the important points in your assignment.

Strategy 2 Cornell Note-taking

Understand It. . . . . . . When you write the important points you read, you will remember the information more easily later. The Cornell Note-taking system uses a chart that will help you record the main ideas and details of your reading.

Good note-taking is not just writing everything you read. Good note-taking requires thought. It is an active process. Notes should focus on the main points. To decide what is important, you must pay attention. Usually, notes do not include the writer's exact words. Notes are clearer if you write them in your own words. When you finish, your notes should give you a good summary of what you just read.

Try It. . . . . The science article on the next page is about whether living things could survive on Mars. Follow along with a student who is using the Cornell Note-taking system while she reads.

Strategy Tip

When you set a purpose for reading, you think about *why* you are reading. You ask yourself what you need to find out. This will help you find the information you need.

Step 1. Preview what you will read.

Look quickly at the title, the subheadings, and any photographs or art you see. If you are reading a book that has a table of contents, preview that too. Read the first and last paragraphs. Ask yourself what the author is trying to tell you. Remember that the writer *wants* you to understand. As you preview, think about what you'll be reading. Think about what you know about the topic. This will help you set a purpose for your reading.

Step 2. Read, then take notes.

When you use the Cornell Note-taking system, you take notes in a special way. Notice that the chart below is divided into two parts. Key words and main points are on the left. Details that explain each idea or evidence that supports it are on the right. Often, titles and subheadings point to key ideas.

Here is how the student began taking notes after she read the article about Mars.

Main Points	Evidence/Details
problems with introducing life to Mars	

Notice that she is focusing on the difficulties of introducing life to Mars. The subheadings have told her that the author is focusing on how hard it would be to live on Mars. The photograph also has made her think of how different Earth and Mars are. Her next step is to reread the article and take notes. Add your own main points and details to this chart after you have read the article.

Main Points	Evidence/Details
problems with introducing life to Mars	distance from Earth very cold how much water? How could you even do it?

Mars, Meet Life

Far away, on Mars, the Red Planet, wheat ripens on farms and oceans teem with life. Lions roar and kittens purr in their owners' laps. The fantasy of life on Mars has inspired artists, scientists, and writers. For some scientists, though, the subject is not just science fiction. They have been working seriously on the possibility of introducing life to Mars.

What's the Problem?

The idea doesn't make sense to some people. First, there is the distance. It could take two years, or much longer, just to get to Mars. Second, the planet is very cold, as much as 60 degrees Celsius *below* zero! Third, no one knows how much water Mars has. Fourth, how could people live there—even if they wanted to?

Answers from Science

Scientists line up to answer the last question. A surprising number of people not only dream of living on Mars, but have detailed ideas about how to turn Mars into an outer-space paradise. One by one, let's look at the problems and how scientists plan to solve them.

Cornell Note-taking

Vocabulary Tip

You may be able to define *propulsion* by thinking about other forms of the word. For example, *propel* means "to move something forward." Knowing *propel* can help you define *propulsion*.

Except in the movies, no one yet has figured out how to travel at warp speed. A journey to Mars could take years. Some scientists suggest using solar-powered engines instead of the **propulsion** systems of the space shuttles. That would save money, they argue. Power from the sun would be a cheap fuel that wouldn't run out. Scientists also say that developing a hibernation system for space travelers is possible. Years in space could be spent in dreamless sleep.

Another problem is that Mars has no liquid water. It has only ice. Mirrors could direct the sun's heat to the ice caps at the planet's poles, scientists say. That could melt the ice and create the water all living things need. Releasing the carbon dioxide in Mars's soil could create a greenhouse effect that would lead to a warmer atmosphere. Some people even suggest finding ice asteroids and directing them to Mars to add to the water supply.

The surface of Mars recorded by the Viking 1 spaceship

The Moral Question

Some people think the idea of introducing Earth's life forms to Mars is wrong. Life forms may already live on Mars. What right do humans have to grab another planet? On the other hand, argue some scientists, what if no life exists on Mars and never has? We would just be using another planet, not stealing someone else's home.

Scientists from Earth might be able to use Mars as a kind of laboratory. They could experiment with ways to make sure Earth never becomes a barren planet. They could try ways to stop global warming and to clean up Earth's polluted oceans.

Certainly, people won't be moving to Mars soon. Scientists dream, but they aren't yet ready to schedule regular trips to Mars. As technology develops, sending crews to Mars might become possible. However, more people will have more opinions on the subject. The question of what to do with Mars may become the environmental debate of the 21st century.

Step 3. Summarize what you have read.

Look at the notes you took. Do your main points mention the problems of living on Mars? Do your details give enough information to help you understand each problem?

Your next step is to write a summary of the article. Your summary should include all of these main points in the article as well as the information that explains them. Here is the way the student began her summary:

> Summary
>
> Scientists are working on the idea of introducing life to Mars. There are some major problems to solve, though: distance, temperature, water, and the moral question of whether to do it. Scientists may be able to solve the problem of distance by . . .

Strategy Tip

Before you begin your summary, review your notes. Underline or highlight important words or phrases. That will help you remember them.

Now write your own summary of the article on the lines below.

_____

_____

_____

_____

_____

Step 4. Review what you have learned.

Did you really learn the information in the article? Test yourself. Fold your notes so that only the main points show. Can you remember the details you wrote? If you can't, review your summary.

Apply It. . . . . Try the Cornell Note-taking method on a reading assignment you have. Make sure you ask questions as you preview. Then read the assignment. When you have finished reading, divide your paper into two columns. Take notes on the main points and evidence or details that support them. Finally, write a summary to help you review what you have learned.

Strategy 3   KWL Plus

Understand It...... Active readers approach reading by thinking about what they are going to read and why they are reading. The KWL Plus strategy (**K**now, **W**ant to Know, **L**earned) is one way to do that. First, you think about and write what you already know about a topic. Then you write what you want to know. After you read, you write what you have learned. To help you remember what you read, you write a summary of what you have learned. The summary is the **P**lus part of the strategy.

Try It............. The selection on the next page is about the American writer Mark Twain. Follow along with a student as he uses the KWL Plus strategy to understand what he is reading.

Step 1. Write what you know about the topic.

Thinking about what you know focuses your mind on what you will be reading. It will help you connect what you know and what you learn. Here's what the student thought as he previewed the selection:

I think I've read some things by Mark Twain. I know—he wrote Huckleberry Finn. *Let's see, what else do I know? Well, I know Twain spent time on the Mississippi River.*

Look at what the student wrote in the K column of his KWL chart. Then add at least two things you know to the list about Mark Twain, *Huckleberry Finn,* or the Mississippi River.

> **Strategy Tip**
>
> As you fill out the K section, stop and brainstorm for a few seconds. You may know more than you think about the topic.

K (What I know)	W (What I want to know)	L (What I've learned)
Wrote *Huckleberry Finn* Spent time on the Mississippi River		

> **Strategy Tip**
>
> Be sure some of your W questions begin with *why* or *how.*

Step 2. Write what you want to learn.

The questions you write can help you focus your reading. They can also help you organize your thinking as you read. Here is what the student thought:

I want to know more about Mark Twain's life. When was he born? Where did he grow up? What else did he write?

In the W column of his KWL chart, the student listed some questions he wanted to answer about Mark Twain. Add at least two questions you want to answer about Twain.

K (What I know)	W (What I want to know)	L (What I've learned)
Wrote *Huckleberry Finn* Spent time on the Mississippi River	When was Twain born? Where did he live? What books did he write?	

Step 3. Write what you learn.

After you read the selection, write the important facts you learned in the L column of the KWL chart that follows the article. Pay special attention to writing the facts that answer the questions you asked.

Mark Twain, from Pilothouse to Pen

He set type and mined silver. He worked as a newspaper reporter. All Samuel Clemens really wanted to do, though, was to pilot a steamboat on the Mississippi River. He probably would have spent his whole life on the river. However, the steamboat era ended after the Civil War (1861–1865). Clemens needed to find another job. The end of the steamboats was the beginning of Mark Twain, one of this country's best-known writers.

When the river pilot became a writer, he took a pen name that showed his love of the Mississippi River. Samuel Clemens became "Mark Twain." To a river pilot, *twain* means "two **fathoms**." A fathom is 6 feet. River pilots always needed to know how deep the water was. They would call out "mark twain" to let others know the water was 12 feet deep. This was deep enough to keep a boat from running aground. One of Twain's best-known books, *Life on the Mississippi,* tells the stories of Twain's days as Samuel Clemens, the riverboat pilot.

Samuel Clemens was born in Florida, Mississippi, in 1835. The Clemens family moved to Hannibal, Missouri, a port on the Mississippi River, when Samuel was four. At age 16, he started setting type and writing sketches for the *Hannibal Journal.* The first short story he signed as Mark Twain, "The Celebrated Jumping Frog of Calaveras County,"

Vocabulary Tip

When you see an unfamiliar word, try looking at nearby words for a definition. You'll notice that *fathom* is defined in the next sentence.

was published in 1865. Before long, Twain was the most famous comic writer of his day.

Twain's novel *The Adventures of Huckleberry Finn* has become an American classic. It is a story of childhood and growing up. A young boy named Huck and an enslaved man named Jim run away together on a homemade raft. During their journey on the Mississippi River, they both learn about life. Huck comes to see that slavery is wrong. Jim learns that even if he becomes free, he will probably face racism in many places. Huck and Jim's adventure takes place just before the Civil War. One issue the North and South fought over was whether people in the South had the right to own slaves.

American novelist Mark Twain, in a portrait by Frank Larson

Huckleberry Finn was published in 1885, and people have argued about it ever since. Although people all over the country bought the book, many people felt children shouldn't read it. The public library in Concord, Massachusetts, banned the book soon after it was published. A librarian named E. L. Pearson said that by 1907, libraries everywhere were taking *The Adventures of Huckleberry Finn* off their shelves. Other people were outraged by the friendship between a white person and an African American. They said the character Jim was too "heroic." In the mid- to late 1950s, people working for civil rights attacked the book. They said that it was racist and that Jim was a stereotype of an African American.

People still disagree about *Huckleberry Finn.* In 1997, the American Library Association listed it as one of the most challenged or banned books in the country. Challenged means that people have tried to remove the book from schools and libraries.

Mark Twain probably would not be surprised that the debate over *Huckleberry Finn* goes on. He believed in the American ideal of freedom to speak and tell the truth as he saw it. He wrote about the great variety of people in the United States, and he never missed a chance to poke fun at people he thought were wrong or foolish.

Strategy Tip

The first sentence of this paragraph might make you wonder why people have fought over *Huckleberry Finn.* Add this question to your KWL chart. You can use the information in this paragraph to answer that question.

In the L column of the KWL chart on the next page are some notes the student wrote after reading the selection. Add your own notes to the chart.

K (What I know)	W (What I want to know)	L (What I've learned)
Wrote *Huckleberry Finn* Spent time on the Mississippi River	When was Twain born? Where did he live? What books did he write?	Born in 1835 Grew up in Hannibal, Missouri Wrote *Life on the Mississippi* and *Huckleberry Finn*

Strategy Tip

Use your completed KWL chart to help you write a summary of what you have learned.

Step 4. Write a summary of what you have learned.

Writing a summary ensures that you remember what you have read. Summarizing can also help you figure out the most important points of a selection. Here's how the student began his summary. Use this beginning as a model to write your own summary.

> **Summary**
>
> This biography of Mark Twain talks about how he did many things before he was a writer. His favorite job was being a steamboat pilot on the Mississippi . . .

Apply It . . . .

Try the KWL strategy on a reading assignment you have. First, think about the topic of the assignment. What do you know about it? What would you like to learn about it?

Next, draw a KWL chart on a sheet of paper. Before you begin reading, fill in the K column with what you already know about the topic. Then fill in the W column with things you want to learn from your reading.

After you read, fill in the L column with the answers to your questions. Then review your KWL chart to make sure all of your questions are answered. Finally, use your chart to write a summary of what you have read. You can use this summary to review what you learned and to study for a test.

Strategy 4 Concept Building

Understand It . . . . . . The reading strategy called Concept Building is especially useful for math and science readings. It is based on the idea that when you read these subjects, you must know one concept, or idea, before you move on. For example, if you can't add, you'll have trouble learning multiplication. When you use Concept Building, you learn each term or concept as it is presented. Then, review what you have learned. This step ensures that you understand your reading.

Try It . . . . The selection on the next page explains the process of sleep. Before you read, preview to see what it will be about. You will notice that the writing focuses on one main concept: the two kinds of sleep.

When you use the Concept Building strategy, you preview to find the main concept and write it. Then you read the selection. Next, you write a definition of the concept and the evidence or details that explain the concept. In math or science, you might write the steps of a process or operation. In the last step, you review what you have learned to make sure you understand the concept.

Follow along with a student who is using the Concept Building strategy to understand the selection about sleep.

Step 1. Preview to find the main concept.

No matter what you read, preview the selection before you read. When you use the Concept Building strategy, you look for specific things. You look for words in boldface, or dark, type. These words often are followed by a definition or explanation. Also, look for other signs, like bullets (dots in a list), numbered lists, information in a box, or an illustration.

To use the Concept Building strategy, the student first drew the chart shown below. Then she thought about the subject and previewed the selection. This is what she thought as she previewed:

Sleep—let's see. I know it has to do with stages. There's the term REM Sleep in boldface type. It must be important. I'll write it in the Concept column. NREM Sleep is also in boldface type. I'll write that too.

Concept	Definition or Formula	Evidence or Steps	Review or Examples
REM sleep			
NREM sleep			

Now preview the selection below. Look for signals like boldface type, lists, and illustrations. Then read the selection. As you read, think about REM and NREM. You might want to highlight or underline any definitions or explanations you see. If you find a new concept in your reading, note it.

Asleep in Seattle . . . and Singapore . . . and Senegal

As different as people are, we all have at least one thing in common. Across the world, people get sleepy when the sun goes down. They find a place to lie down, and they fall asleep.

Research on brain waves shows two kinds of sleep. **REM sleep** (Rapid Eye Movement) is close to wakefulness. **NREM sleep** (Non Rapid Eye Movement) is deeper sleep.

According to researchers, this is what happens when people sleep. First, people go through four stages of NREM sleep.

Stage 1 The person drifts between wakefulness and sleep. Muscles relax. Pulse and breathing become even.

Stage 2 Breathing and heart rate slow.

Stage 3 Breathing and heart rate slow even more. Body temperature and blood pressure drop.

Stage 4 This is the deepest sleep. Muscles relax completely. The sleeper moves little. Waking a person in stage 4 sleep is very difficult. People who say they can "sleep through an earthquake" are talking about stage 4.

During the night, a person goes through all four stages of sleep. When stage 4 is complete, the sleeper reverses the process. He or she returns to stage 3, then stage 2, then back to stage 1. A cycle takes about 70 to 90 minutes.

After that pattern, the sleeper enters REM sleep. This kind of sleep can last from 5 to 15 minutes. While in REM sleep, a person's eyes move quickly back and forth beneath closed eyelids. He or she may twitch or move restlessly.

Throughout the night, the sleeper will repeat the REM–NREM pattern. However, researchers have learned that REM sleep gets longer with each cycle, until REM sleep makes up 20 to 25 percent of sleep time each night.

Vocabulary Tip

The boldface type shows you that the writer is introducing a new concept. Each concept is followed by an explanation written in parentheses.

Concept Building

Step 2. Explain the concept.

The student has already added the REM and NREM concepts to her Concept Building chart. Then she added information to the Definition column. She defined REM sleep. Add your own definition of NREM sleep to this chart. Here is what she thought as she began her chart:

The definitions for REM and NREM sleep are right after the words. I'll write the definitions of these terms in the Definition or Formula column.

Concept	Definition or Formula	Evidence or Steps	Review or Examples
REM sleep	Rapid Eye Movement close to wakefulness		
NREM sleep			

Strategy Tip

The notes you write in the Evidence column should be in your own words. Putting information in your own words helps you remember it.

Step 3. Write the steps or the evidence for the concept.

Now read the selection. After you have read, write the evidence or details that explain each concept in the Evidence or Steps column. Evidence includes any information that helps you understand the concept. For this science selection, the student added the evidence that explained REM and NREM sleep. Add some additional evidence that you found to the chart.

The article gives some facts about REM and NREM sleep. I'll write those facts in the Evidence or Steps column.

Concept	Definition or Formula	Evidence or Steps	Review or Examples
REM sleep	Rapid Eye Movement close to wakefulness	lasts 5 to 15 minutes sleeper's eyes twitch	
NREM sleep		Stage 1: between wakefulness and sleep Stage 2: _____ Stage 3: _____ Stage 4: _____	

Step 4. Review what you have learned.

Reviewing helps you make sure you understand what you've read. That's what the last column in the Concept Building chart is for. In science, the last column may be a summary. In math, you might try other problems to see if you understand how to use the concept. This is the way the student began filling out the last column in her chart.

Concept

REM sleep

NREM sleep

Definition or Formula

Rapid Eye Movement close to wakefulness

Evidence or Steps

lasts 5 to 15 minutes

sleeper's eyes twitch

Stage 1: between wakefulness and sleep

Stage 2: _____

Stage 3: _____

Stage 4: _____

Review or Examples

In REM sleep, the sleeper's eyes move quickly.

Apply It . . . . Try the Concept Building strategy on a reading assignment you have that presents one or two concepts. First, preview to find the concept. Then read, looking for a definition of the concept. If you are allowed to write in the book, you might highlight or underline important information. If you are not allowed to write in the book, jot down a few notes to help you locate the information later.

When you have finished reading, write any information you found that explains the concept in the Evidence or Steps column. Finally, write a review of what you have learned in the Review or Examples column. Test yourself to be sure you *do* understand. Try writing a summary. If the concept is a formula, try using the formula on another problem.

Unit 2
Reading in Language Arts

Diaries and adventure tales are language arts reading. So are instructions on how to write a letter of complaint. Language arts reading is many things. When you read for fun, you are probably reading in language arts. In school, you may read biographies and essays. You also may read to learn skills such as how to identify an adjective or how to use punctuation. Language arts reading covers a wide variety of topics.

How Language Arts Reading Is Organized

Although there are many kinds of readings in language arts, these readings are organized in a few basic ways. If you can recognize how a reading is organized, you will know what to expect. You will be prepared to learn new information. When you preview, look for clues to how the reading is organized. Here are a few of the patterns you will see in language arts readings.

Main Idea and Details. Many kinds of language arts reading are written about a single topic. In this pattern, everything in the article is connected to the main topic. In an English textbook, the topic may be how to write an essay. In a magazine article, the topic may be auto racing. When you see this pattern, you know that there will be many details that support or explain the topic.

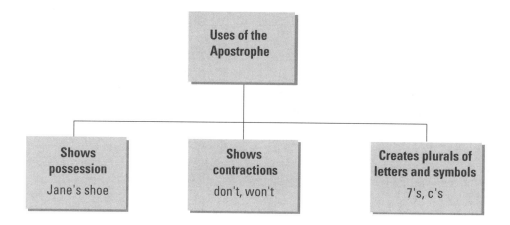

Sequence of Events. This type of organization is common in diaries, true-life adventure stories, and biographies. When you are previewing, look for dates. They are easy to recognize, and they tell you that the reading is organized in chronological, or time, order.

Moss's Journey

| **Sept. 1**
Moss sets out on a journey | **Sept. 30**
Crosses prairie | **Oct. 15**
Crosses mountain pass | **Nov. 1**
Spends week in blizzard on other side of pass | **Nov. 15**
Reaches lake and family |

Cause and Effect. This structure is common in all types of reading. You may see it in novels. In a true-adventure story, you may notice that one event causes another event. When you see this pattern, draw a series of boxes. These boxes show you how one event causes another event. That can help you understand how events work together to make a chain.

Parkertown Flood

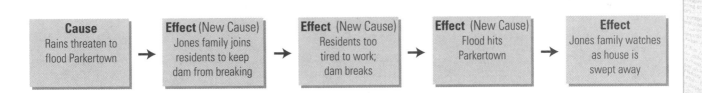

| **Cause**
Rains threaten to flood Parkertown | → | **Effect** (New Cause)
Jones family joins residents to keep dam from breaking | → | **Effect** (New Cause)
Residents too tired to work; dam breaks | → | **Effect** (New Cause)
Flood hits Parkertown | → | **Effect**
Jones family watches as house is swept away |

Getting the Most from Your Reading

If you can recognize the way a reading is organized, you will better understand what you read. You will be able to think about what kind of information might be next and how all the points in the reading fit together. Drawings like the ones on these two pages can show you these patterns. Thinking about how a reading is organized can help you understand—and remember—what you read.

Magazine Article:
The True Story of Blue Jeans

Understand It......

Hint
You can review the KWL Plus strategy on page 12.

This article discusses a subject you probably know something about: blue jeans. Because jeans are such a familiar subject, using the KWL Plus strategy probably makes sense for you. Try it as you read this article.

Think about what you know about blue jeans. Then think about the title. The title uses the word *true*. Is there a *false* story about blue jeans?

Try It..............

Begin using the KWL strategy by previewing the article. You'll notice some dates. Maybe the story is a history, written in chronological, or time, order. You might learn some facts.

Once you have finished previewing, draw a KWL chart like the one below on a separate piece of paper. Write what you know in the K column. Try asking *when, how,* and *why* to develop your questions for the W column. Keep these questions in mind as you read. When you have finished reading, you will write what you learned in the L column. Then you will summarize the article.

Strategy Tip

Don't write *everything* you know about jeans in the K column. Preview the article to see what topics it discusses. That will help you ask questions that the article will answer.

K (What I know)	W (What I want to know)	L (What I've learned)

The True Story of Blue Jeans

On average, every American owns seven pairs of jeans. He or she also has a denim jacket, four pairs of jean shorts, and two denim shirts. Americans buy more than 512 million pairs of jeans every year. How did work pants evolve into a huge, international fashion basic?

Blue jeans have a romantic history. In 1853, Levi Strauss, a Bavarian immigrant living in New York City, moved to the West to get in on the California gold rush. He began selling items miners needed, such as clothing and tents. In 1872, he got a letter from Jacob Davis. Davis had invented a process for riveting pockets onto pants. The idea sounded good to Strauss. The two men went into business together. Strauss called the new trousers "waist-high overalls." That made them different from the familiar bib overalls of the day. Miners loved the new pants. The pants could take the punishment their hardworking owners **dished out**. When the jeans finally wore out, miners stuffed them into cracks in the mines to stop rock slides.

Over the years, jeans evolved. At first, the pants had only one back pocket. There was a pocket for a watch and suspender buttons.

Vocabulary Tip

You know the word *dish* as a noun, as in a "dish of ice cream." *Dish* can be a verb too. It can mean "to put something on a plate" or "to give something out." Here, the miners are "giving out" punishment to their sturdy pants.

In 1886, the leather patch featuring two horses was added. The horses trying to pull apart a pair of jeans. In 1922, belt loops were added. Lady Levis, the first jeans for women, appeared in 1935. Finally, in 1937, the company started covering the rivets so they wouldn't scratch chairs or saddles. Thirty years later, the rivets disappeared from the back pockets.

Jeans Explode in Popularity

Until the end of World War II, Levis were sold only in 11 western states. World War II, though, made jeans popular overseas. U.S. soldiers sold them to pilots from England. That was the beginning of jeans as an international fashion statement.

Cowboys—and movie cowboys—had always worn jeans. The pants became an emblem of the Wild West. Jeans became the essence of cool in the 1950s. At that time, James Dean, who was a very cool actor, wore jeans in his movies. Marilyn Monroe contributed to the history of jeans too. She wore them in a famous photograph.

Many school officials banned jeans in the classroom in the 1950s. Jeans meant "motorcycle boys." Students wearing jeans were rebels with an eye for trouble. Nothing could stop the popularity of the rugged trousers, though. In 1958, a newspaper reported that "about 90 percent of American youths wear jeans everywhere except in bed and in church."

In the 1960s, the image of jeans as the clothing of rebellion grew. College students wore them to classes and to protest marches. In the decades since, the appeal of jeans has never really faded.

Jeans Grow into the 21st Century

Even though the popularity of jeans continued to grow, the material itself faded. In the 1980s and 1990s, softer, pre-washed denim was in style. Students began buying jeans that had been treated so they looked worn. Jeans were often washed with stones to make them look old. One jeans company has tried nearly everything. It has washed jeans with everything from shredded bottle caps to golf balls, rope, and wood. As the year 2000 nears, the trend is in the opposite direction: to keep the fabric looking stiff and dark blue. In other words, jeans look new again.

Blue jeans no longer sell for $1.25, as the first jeans did. However, almost everyone you know probably owns a pair of jeans. The jeans may not be Levis, though. Dozens of designers and manufacturers fill the stores with their brands. Everyone seems to have blue jeans. Today, you can even buy a $1,500 ball gown made of silk that looks like denim.

The popularity of blue jeans shows no signs of slipping. They are still the "basic pants" of people in the United States and in many other parts of the world. American clothing industries love blue jeans. The pants that the miners loved are still loved worldwide today.

Strategy Tip

Think about what you know about styles in jeans today. List this information in the K column of your KWL chart.

Magazine Article:
The True Story of Blue Jeans

When you finish reading the article, complete the L column of your KWL chart. Then look back at your W questions to see if they were answered. Finally, use your KWL chart to write a summary of the article.

Apply It. . . . . To check your understanding of the article, circle the best answer to each question below.

Test Tip

More than one of the choices for question 1 might be *true*, but the correct answer is the choice that states the *main* point of the article.

1. The main point of this article is that
   a. everyone owns blue jeans.
   b. jeans are a well-known American brand of clothing.
   c. jeans are an American invention that continues to be popular today.
   d. jeans were invented in America.

2. In the "Jeans Explode in Popularity" section, *essence* means
   a. basic nature.
   b. scent.
   c. feeling.
   d. importance.

3. You can conclude that school officials who banned jeans thought
   a. students who wore them were looking for trouble.
   b. jeans would make students rebellious in school.
   c. schools should have dress codes.
   d. jeans might lead to motorcycle gang wars.

4. One thing that has remained true of jeans throughout their history is that
   a. they have always been signs of rebellion.
   b. people have always thought of them as cool.
   c. they have changed with the times.
   d. they have always looked the same.

Use the lines below to write your answers for numbers 5 and 6. Your KWL chart and summary will help you.

5. How have Americans' feelings about jeans changed from the time they were first made to today? Write your answer as a summary.

_____

_____

6. Suppose you are a high-school student in the 1950s. Your school has banned jeans. Write to your principal and explain why students should be allowed to wear jeans. Use examples and evidence from the article in your argument.

_____

_____

Biography:
The Quiet Crusader

Understand It......

You might not know the man the writer calls "the quiet crusader," but you already know at least one fact about him. He is someone who is important enough or interesting enough to have a biography written about him.

Hint

You can review the Cornell Note-taking strategy on page 8.

You also know that biographies are often organized in predictable ways. Some biographies follow a person's life from birth to death. Others are organized around the themes or events. For example, a biography of Thomas Jefferson might focus on his writing the Declaration of Independence.

Try It..............

Try using the Cornell Note-taking strategy with this biography. When you preview it, look at the title, the photograph, and the subheadings. Read the first and last paragraphs and all of the topic sentences. You now know that Moses has been involved in the Civil Rights Movement and something called the Algebra Project.

On a separate sheet of paper, draw a Cornell Note-taking chart like the one shown below. After you read, note the most important facts in the Main Points column. List support for those Main Points in the Evidence/Details column. Then write a summary of what you have learned.

Strategy Tip

You can also make a Cornell Note-taking chart by folding a piece of paper. Fold the paper so that the Main Points column takes about 1/3 of the paper's width. The Evidence/Details column should take about 2/3 of the paper's width.

Main Points	**Evidence/Details**

The Quiet Crusader

In 1961, three African American men walked slowly toward the Amite County courthouse in Mississippi. Two were on their way to register to vote. Robert Moses was there to help. Three white men blocked their way. "Where are you going?" one asked. "To register the men to vote," Moses said. "No, you aren't," the man said. He jabbed at Moses's head with the handle of his knife.

Moses staggered. The man hit him again and again. "We can't let something like this stop us," Moses said. The three walked on. Blood stained Moses's white shirt. The clerk at the courthouse gasped at the sight of Moses. He closed the office. Those who wanted to stop Moses had won—for that day. Eventually, though, Moses and his fellow crusaders for voting rights would succeed.

Biography:
The Quiet Crusader

Strategy Tip

A new subheading often signals that a new Main Point is being introduced.

Robert Moses has never talked much about that day or about the part he played in the Civil Rights Movement. His actions have spoken for him.

The New Civil Rights

Moses still thinks that working for African Americans' rights is important. His target has changed, though. Moses spends his time on math education and the Algebra Project. He believes learning math can help African Americans gain economic success.

Moses knows education can help children improve their chances in life. Education helped him. When he was a child, his family lived in a housing project. Moses attended a high school for gifted students. When he finished college, he started work on his doctorate at Harvard University. He was forced to quit school to support his ill father. When the Civil Rights Movement began, Moses was teaching high school in New York City. In the 1960s, he spent his summers in the South, helping African Americans gain their voting rights.

Twenty years later, Moses became dissatisfied with his daughter's math education. Math, Moses says, is the key to a good future. Without algebra, students can't take the math courses they need for college. People who don't go to college have great difficulty getting jobs that pay well.

Creating the Algebra Project

Strategy Tip

Photographs chosen for a biography usually show you something about the person's character or actions. What does this photograph show you about Robert Moses?

Moses designed a new way of teaching. He based his method on his ideas about how people learn. A student looks at an algebra problem taken from real life. Then he or she puzzles out a solution with friends and writes about it. Finally, the student writes the answer in mathematical terms.

Robert Moses with Algebra Project kids

In the beginning, some educators were unsure about Moses's approach. Former critics now agree that the method works. Students learn to use algebra to solve everyday problems. That helps them remember what they learn. The Algebra Project reaches thousands of students across the country.

To Moses, the link between the work he does today and his civil rights work in Mississippi is clear. Without votes, African Americans in 1960 lacked political power. Without college, African Americans of today have limited chances to have economic power.

Vocabulary Tip

In English, words often have more than one meaning. You probably know one definition of *exercise*: "to work out." That's a clue to the meaning of *exercise* as it is used here.

In 1960, in his quiet way, Robert Moses helped African Americans **exercise** their right to vote. Today, he helps their sons and daughters exercise their right to have equal economic opportunity.

Now look over your notes. Did you note the key ideas in the Main Points column? Did you note the details or evidence for these ideas in the Evidence/Details column? Use your Cornell chart to help you write a summary of the biography of Robert Moses.

Apply It. . . . . To check your understanding of the biography, circle the best answer to each question below.

1. Before the Civil Rights Movement, African Americans in Mississippi did not vote because
   a. it was against the law.
   b. whites would not let them register to vote.
   c. they didn't think the candidates would help them.
   d. they did not think voting mattered.

2. How does the Algebra Project help students learn?
   a. Students work together to solve a real-life math problem.
   b. Students are taught study skills.
   c. Students work closely with their teacher to learn algebra.
   d. Students study algebra on computers.

3. The word *exercise* in the last paragraph of the biography means
   a. work out.
   b. lose.
   c. use.
   d. work hard.

4. Moses believes algebra is important for economic success because
   a. algebra is needed to do many high-paying jobs.
   b. employers look for students who have taken algebra.
   c. algebra is needed to earn good grades in college.
   d. algebra is needed to get into college, which helps students get high-paying jobs.

Use the lines below to write your answers for numbers 5 and 6. You can use your Cornell Note-taking chart to help you.

5. What qualities does Moses have that helped him succeed as a leader? Give evidence from the article to support your answer.

_____

_____

Test Tip

When you compare, you find similarities. When you contrast, you find differences.

6. Compare and contrast the voting rights drive and the Algebra Project. Use examples from the biography in your answer.

_____

_____

Lesson 3

Personal Letter: Caught in the Blitz

Hint

You can review the PACA strategy on page 4.

Understand It...... Look at the headline and photograph that appear with this letter. Then preview the letter. You'll probably have a good idea of what the subject is: World War II. You may know some things about World War II. Because all these things can give you clues to what you might read, the PACA strategy can help you get the most from this letter.

Try It............... Draw a PACA chart like the one below on a separate sheet of paper. After you preview the letter, make your predictions. The writer put an address and a date on the letter, so you know where and when it was written. Look closely at the photo. Does it give you an idea about what "the Blitz" was? You can probably predict that a *blitz* is a very destructive event.

Now read the letter. After you read, review your predictions. Add a check mark in the small box if you can confirm a prediction. If you find information you didn't predict, write it in the Predictions column and add a star to the small box. Cross out or revise predictions that were wrong. Then write the evidence for your predictions in the Support column.

Strategy Tip

You might not be able to make many predictions about this reading. Thinking about predictions, whether you can make any or not, makes you more aware of the subject. Make sure, though, that you note the important facts you did not predict.

Predictions	Support

Vocabulary Tip

Although you might not know the word *drone* in this sentence, you can guess that a *drone* is a sound.

Caught in the Blitz

London, England
May 13, 1941

Dear Jimmy,

I've been so involved in my troubles. But until I got your note from Boston, I didn't realize how worried you might be about what's going on here. Our school days together seem so long ago. I have so much to say that I hardly know where to start. Perhaps the easiest way is to start at the beginning: September 7, 1940. That's when it all began.

You probably know that Hitler decided to start bombing London then. He figured he could easily bring us to our knees. He didn't—or at least he hasn't yet. If things don't change soon, though, I don't know what will happen.

I remember the shock of hearing the **drone** of the planes from far away and then hearing the explosions. They seemed endless. Mum,

Dad, Jenny, and I had taken shelter in a closet on the ground floor of our house. We could still hear the sounds, though.

At the end of that first night, I came out of the house just as dawn was breaking. All around me was rubble. The day before, there had been flower boxes and tidy stores and buildings—and now, nothing. Piles of silent bricks, glass everywhere, and pieces of broken walls that were jagged and smoking. The other thing I remember, besides the unbelievable destruction, was the sound—or lack of it. The city was almost totally silent, particularly right at dawn. I found out the Germans had dropped 600 *tons* of bombs on London that night.

The next night, it was the same, and the next and the next. We started spending the night in the Underground, after the trains had stopped for the day. One problem with staying there was the people all around us. Some acted crazy. One man just started cackling one night, and no one could get him to stop. Sleep was impossible.

After a while, people began calling the nightly bombings "the Blitz." What strikes me is how we got used to it. You can get used to just about anything. For the next two months, Hitler bombed us—*every single night.* Everyone knew someone who had died. Whole families decided not to take shelter or were homeless or had lost people. I could see why people didn't take shelter. The lines to get into the Underground stations began forming early in the day. After a while, I thought, "Well, what will happen will happen. I could just as easily get hit here." Of course, it wasn't true, but the longer it went on, the more we started thinking, "Well, nothing has happened so far, so. . . ."

One night, we decided to stay in our house. I don't think any of us slept all night. The whining of the airplanes was terrible. My stomach felt like one big knot. The sound just wouldn't go away. Then the orange would light the sky, and I'd sometimes see flames.

Officials examine extensive damage caused by a WWII bombing in London.

The bombing went on and on, and although I never got used to the sound of the whining planes, we started pretending that nothing was happening. We even started going out at night.

We found a restaurant we really liked. We could go there and forget what was happening. They played loud music. I suppose that was to cover up the sounds outside.

Strategy Tip

As you preview, look for terms within quotation marks. Here, quotation marks surround the term "the Blitz." What information have you noticed so far about this terrible time?

Strategy Tip

What does this photograph show you about the Blitz? Add a prediction to your PACA chart about what the Blitz was like.

Personal Letter: Caught in the Blitz

One night, a bomb hit the restaurant. It seemed like it had fallen right on my head. I have to try to describe it for you. It might be good for me. I've really tried not to think about it, but I dream about it.

One minute, we were partying and then nothing—blackness. The explosion knocked me out. When I came to, I was confused. I couldn't figure out why I was slumped on the floor, covered with dust, and where the walls had gone. I couldn't understand why I was not moving. I felt sticky. It was completely quiet. Then I saw a flame nearby and another, and suddenly I knew what was happening. We'd been hit.

The stickiness was blood. It was all over my shirt. I just sat there, looking at it. I had no desire to move. I felt like I was watching a movie. Of course, eventually ambulances and nurses came. They moved me to an open space outside where many other people were all laid out. Someone stitched up my arm. That was where the blood was coming from.

I'm fine now. I no longer think the bombs will stop falling. They never do. Three nights ago, more than 2,000 fires broke out across London. The drone was intense that night. I don't think I'll ever hear a plane again without looking for a place to hide.

Yours,

Jeremy

When you finish reading the letter, look over your PACA chart. Did you find information that confirmed your predictions? If not, revise your predictions or add new ones. Clear PACA notes can help you review the important points the writer of the letter made.

Apply It. . . . . To check your understanding of the letter, circle the best answer to each question below.

1. Jeremy wrote the letter to Jimmy to
   a. let Jimmy know he is fine.
   b. make his American friend feel sorry for him.
   c. explain what is happening during the Blitz.
   d. explain to Jimmy why his country is at war.

2. Jeremy thinks he will never be able to hear another plane without looking for a place to hide because
   a. it will remind him of London.
   b. it will remind him of listening to the German planes landing nearby.
   c. it will remind him how much he misses his friend.
   d. it will remind him of the bombings.

3. In this letter, the *Underground* is
   a. a bomb shelter.
   b. a subway or transportation system.
   c. anywhere people can get away from the bombs.
   d. a basement.

4. Which choice best describes what Jeremy says at the end of the letter?
   a. He says that he wants to leave London.
   b. He says that his family was killed in the bombing.
   c. He says that he realizes the bombings will continue.
   d. He says that he is happy to still be with his family.

5. Jeremy tells about the bomb falling on the restaurant mainly because
   a. he thinks if he tells the story he won't have nightmares about it.
   b. he wants Jimmy to send food.
   c. he wants to tell Jimmy that the Blitz isn't that bad.
   d. he is trying to show Jimmy the terrible times he's seen.

Use the lines below to write your answers for numbers 6 and 7. You can use your PACA chart and your notes to help you.

6. What does the letter tell you about the relationship between Jeremy and Jimmy?

_____

_____

_____

_____

7. What is the worst part of the Blitz for Jeremy? Explain your answer with examples from the letter.

_____

_____

_____

_____

Lesson 4

Essay: Jazz, An American Art Form

Understand It......

Hint
You can review the Cornell Note-taking strategy on page 8.

You might have heard of jazz. You might even be able to recognize it when you hear it. You might not know much about the musical form, though. Taking notes using the Cornell Note-taking method will help you keep track of the new information you learn.

Try It..............

Preview the essay to get an idea of what the main points are. The title says that jazz is American, so that fact could be important. While you read, you may want to think about why the author described jazz as American. Think about the words *art form* too. You may learn something technical.

Use the drawing below as a model for your Cornell Note-taking chart. Divide your paper into two columns. Make the right column twice as wide as the left. After you read, write main points in the Main Points column. Write the details and supporting evidence in the Evidence/Details column. Then use your Cornell notes to summarize the essay.

Main Points	Evidence/Details

Strategy Tip
Often, the first sentence in a paragraph is the topic sentence. It tells you what the paragraph will be about. When you preview a reading, pay close attention to the topic sentences. They may give you a rough outline of the reading.

Jazz, An American Art Form

Music is an international language. The experiences of all human beings inspire musical forms, and every form contributes to the next. Composers freely borrow from one another. All over the world, people fall in love with the music of other cultures.

Jazz developed in the United States at the beginning of the 20th century. It was the product of many influences. Strains of African American work chants, spirituals, and folk music weave through jazz. Bits of opera and popular songs can be heard in jazz. African American musicians drew on a variety of musical expressions to create something new. Jazz mixes many musical forms.

If jazz has a direct ancestor, it is ragtime. Ragtime, which first appeared in the 1890s, is bright, rhythmic piano music, composed mainly by African Americans. It caught on across America during the "Gay Nineties." Scott Joplin was the best-known ragtime composer and performer. His music became popular again in the 1970s and 1980s.

So what is jazz, anyway? Most people agree that they know it when they hear it. Take the rhythms of ragtime. Add bits and pieces of other forms. Throw in the harmonies of the blues, another African American musical form, and you get jazz. Jazz has **syncopated**, or offbeat, rhythms. Jazz musicians improvise and take musical risks. Some of the best jazz ever written was never written. It was, instead, inspired by the moment. Jazz sometimes happens when a jazz musician stands up and takes the music where his or her spirit leads.

That love of **improvisation**, or composing at the spur of the moment, may be particularly American. Americans have always loved the individualist. Americans admire those who go it alone. They like people who don't play by the rules. Nothing describes jazz better.

The Jazzy New Century

The changes in jazz mirror the changes in 20th-century America. Jazz was born with the new century. Americans were in love with the new, and nothing was newer than jazz.

The decade of the 1920s was known as the "Jazz Age." Jazz became a symbol of the times. The 1920s were also called the "Roaring Twenties." The stock market rose, and times were good. Women expressed rebellion against traditional roles by cutting their hair and wearing short skirts. Jazz resulted from a musical rebellion. Jazz was daring. Jazz fit the age well.

When the Great Depression began in the 1930s, the Jazz Age died. No one was in the mood for wild times or hot music. People couldn't afford to take chances. As the country's mood gradually improved in the late 1930s, the "Swing Era" began. Swing music, though still jazzy, was smooth. Its rhythms were predictable. This big band music was easy to listen to and easy to like. In some ways, it was a relief from the demanding music of the Jazz Age.

World War II caused yet another change in music. Soldiers longing for home and folks at home who missed the soldiers made sentimental music popular. When the soldiers did come home, bop jazz hit its peak. Bop featured fast tempos, soaring flights on the saxophone, and quickly changing harmonies. Post-World War II America was changing quickly. The mood was upbeat—people's spirits soared.

After the war, the world seemed larger. U.S. soldiers had shared their music with people everywhere. In the 1960s and 1970s, people from various countries in South America and Europe began to listen to jazz. Worldwide, musicians added their own musical heritage to the jazz mix. Today, jazz is a truly international form that remains American at its core.

Essay:
Jazz, An American Art Form

After you finish your Cornell chart, make sure you noted all the main points and the evidence that supports each point. Then use your chart to help you summarize the essay.

Apply It. . . . . To check your understanding of the essay, circle the best answer to each question below.

1. What is the writer's main point in this essay?
   a. Jazz is a reflection of African American heritage.
   b. Jazz developed all over the world.
   c. Jazz is the only art form that is from America.
   d. Jazz is a particularly American art form.

2. Which of these choices describes the way the writer explains jazz?
   a. offbeat rhythms, unusual melodies
   b. unusual melodies, improvisation
   c. offbeat rhythms, African American artists
   d. improvisation, offbeat rhythms

3. In the first section of this essay, *syncopated* means
   a. offbeat.
   b. jazzy.
   c. improvised.
   d. ragtime.

4. According to the writer, the Swing Era happened because
   a. people were in the mood for demanding music.
   b. the country had just entered a Depression and wanted to feel good.
   c. people wanted to listen to music that was not demanding.
   d. no one was in the mood for real jazz.

Test Tip

Question 5 asks about a writer's attitude, which is also called *tone*. The correct answer will describe the way the writer seems to feel about the subject.

5. Which of these words best describes the writer's attitude toward jazz?
   a. disapproving
   b. uninterested
   c. enthusiastic
   d. confused

Use the lines below to write your answers for numbers 6 and 7. You can use your Cornell notes to help you.

6. Contrast the Jazz Age with the Swing Era. Explain how the writer thinks each form of music was related to its time.

_____

_____

7. Summarize why the writer thinks that jazz is an American art form.

_____

_____

Lesson 5

True-Adventure: Iditarod Woman

Understand It......

In this adventure story, you will learn about an unusual and demanding race, the Iditarod. To aid your understanding of the story, use the KWL Plus strategy.

You may know more than you think about the subject. Look at the photograph and read the caption. You'll see that a woman named Susan Butcher and a dog have won a sled-dog race. Next, preview the story. Use what you know and what you learn from previewing to prepare to read.

Try It..............

The graphic below shows a KWL chart. Use it as a model to make your own chart on a separate sheet of paper. Write what you know about sled-dog racing in the K column. Now think about what you would like to know about this topic. Where does the race happen? Who is Susan Butcher? Why does she race? Write your questions in the W column. After you read, fill in the L column. Then use your KWL chart to write a summary of what you've learned.

Strategy Tip

The subheadings tell you that the writer will first discuss Butcher's success, then how she became a sled-dog racer. Use this information to add to your KWL chart.

K (What I know)	W (What I want to know)	L (What I've learned)

Vocabulary Tip

To define *whiteout*, think about the Alaskan landscape. What might cause a whiteout? What might a whiteout look like?

Iditarod Woman

This time, Susan Butcher thought, she would surely win the Iditarod. The Alaskan sled-dog race tests every musher and every musher's team of dogs. The racers face almost two weeks of terrifyingly cold weather and the hazards that go with it. **Whiteouts** are common. Racers lose their way and get turned around. They can become confused in the white blankness that faces them. Even so, Butcher set off confidently, because she was sure that she would win. She also thought her time would be fast. The course was fast because the snow had been packed into a slick surface.

Butcher braced herself. The 1986 race began. She was on her way. At sunset, Butcher and her dogs were flying as they came to a fork in the twisted trail. At one critical turn, Butcher lost control. The sled smacked into one tree after another. Butcher couldn't hang on. Helplessly, she watched as sled and dogs raced ahead.

After a stunned second, Butcher began running. When she finally caught up, she calmed her dogs and assessed the damage. She held her breath. The dogs were fine. Was the sled OK? If not, the race might be over for Butcher and her team. Carefully, she ran her hands over the

True-Adventure:
Iditarod Woman

sled. It was fine. Although Butcher was bruised and her clothes were ripped, she could continue.

Butcher got back on the sled. Soon, she and her dogs were through Rainy Pass. They were the first team over the highest point on the Iditarod Trail. Flying down the pass, Butcher streaked through trees and onto a frozen lake. Suddenly, one of her dogs fell through the ice. Just as quickly, Butcher grabbed an ax and chopped until she made a hole large enough for the dog to climb out. It shook off the ice, and the team continued.

Nearing the Finish

The race was nearly two weeks old, and the end of the trail was near. Butcher was **neck and neck** with two mushers and their teams. One was Joe Garnie, a Native American musher. The other was Rick Swenson, an experienced racer with several wins to his credit. Garnie took the lead. Butcher took it back. Swenson stayed close behind. As the teams raced toward Nome, Butcher and her team heard the fire siren that signaled the end was near.

Vocabulary Tip

Sometimes familiar words can form unfamiliar phrases. You can understand *neck and neck* by thinking of what it might mean in context. *Neck and neck* means "even with."

Butcher whistled to her team, urging the dogs forward. Despite their exhaustion, despite almost two weeks on the trail, the dogs responded. The sled leaped ahead. Just after midnight, Butcher and her team entered the glare of television cameras in Nome. She had won the Iditarod with the fastest time ever: 11 days, 15 hours, and 6 minutes.

Strategy Tip

This photograph might give you information for both the K and W sections of your KWL chart. You might want to ask a *how* question about the Iditarod race.

Sled dog "Granite" with owner Susan Butcher after winning the Iditarod Trail Sled Dog Race

During the next four years, Butcher won three more Iditarods. She came in second in the other race. The Iditarod became a well-known race. People everywhere had heard of Susan Butcher and her dogs. They marveled that she could continue to win such a difficult race. For Butcher, it was nothing unusual—she had been defying expectations all her life.

Getting Ready

As an eight-year-old child in Boston, Butcher had written an essay that began, "I hate the city." In her teens, she discovered a deep love for dogs—and huskies in particular.

When she grew up, Butcher moved to Alaska—about as far from the city as she could get. She had read an article about a new race. It was to be called the Iditarod Trail Sled Dog Race, or the Last Great Race on Earth. During Alaska's gold rush in the early 1900s, the Iditarod Trail had been a freight route. *Iditarod*, which means "far distant place," was a stop on the trail. The race course would be 1,049 miles (1,688 kilometers) long and would run from Anchorage to Nome. It would cross two mountain ranges, as well as forests, farms, and fields. To Butcher, it sounded like heaven.

Getting Set

Butcher began building a dog team. For three winters, she lived 50 miles from civilization. Her cabin had no plumbing and no electricity. She chopped holes through the ice on a nearby stream to get water. Mostly, she trained her dogs. After her third winter in the wild, Butcher entered her first Iditarod. It was 1978.

Her 19th-place finish earned Butcher a share of the prize money. It also gave her the confidence to keep racing. In the years Butcher ran the Iditarod, she tied the record for the most wins—four. She also created new interest in the difficult race. She was a woman competing in an extreme environment. With her ability and toughness, Butcher has become a role model for girls and young women across America. She says she had few role models when she was young. After her success, a T-shirt bearing the words *Alaska, where men are men and women win the Iditarod* became a common sight in Anchorage.

Strategy Tip

If you can't find answers for your questions in the story, you might like to look in a book or magazine, or on the Internet for more information.

Now that you've finished reading the story, look back at your W questions to see if you can answer them. Write the answers in the L column. If you can't answer them with details you remember, reread the story. When you finish your KWL chart, use the L column to write a short summary of what you learned about the Iditarod and Susan Butcher.

Apply It. . . . . To check your understanding of the story, circle the best answer to each question below.

1. Rainy Pass is
   a. the most dangerous place on the Iditarod Trail.
   b. where Susan Butcher lived in the woods in Alaska.
   c. the highest spot on the Iditarod Trail.
   d. the halfway point of the Iditarod Trail.

2. Which of these dangers did Susan Butcher *not* face in the 1986 Iditarod?
   a. a slick snow surface
   b. an out-of-control sled
   c. a dog that broke through ice
   d. rain that turned to ice

True-Adventure:
Iditarod Woman

3. In the first paragraph of this story, *musher* means
   a. a sled dog.
   b. a person racing with sled dogs.
   c. snow that turns soft.
   d. a person who raises sled dogs.

4. The author told about the essay Butcher wrote as an eight-year-old to show that
   a. Butcher had always loved dogs.
   b. Butcher had been interested in the outdoors all her life.
   c. Butcher started to form strong opinions at an early age.
   d. Butcher was a spoiled child.

5. You can infer from this article that Susan Butcher's Iditarod wins
   a. scared other women and kept them from competing.
   b. created interest in the race because she is a woman.
   c. caused many to take up the sport of dog sledding.
   d. were resented by the men she raced against.

Test Tip

Question 5 asks you to *infer*. To infer, you make a judgment based on the facts in the story and your personal knowledge.

Use the lines below to write your answers for numbers 6 and 7. You can use your KWL chart to help you.

6. Using what you learned in this article, how would you describe Susan Butcher?

   _____

   _____

   _____

   _____

7. What do you think the hardest part of the Iditarod would be? Base your answer on details from the article.

   _____

   _____

   _____

   _____

LANGUAGE ARTS

Lesson 6

Essay:
The Beauty of Haiku

Understand It......

Hint
You can review the Concept Building strategy on page 16.

You might have read the form of poetry called *haiku*. This essay explains more about haiku and invites you to create a haiku of your own. Because the essay focuses on one concept—haiku—Concept Building is a good strategy to use to help you understand your reading.

Try It..............

Preview the essay and read the subheadings. They might explain the main concept. They might also describe how haiku are written. The paragraphs that follow each subheading probably give more information.

Then, on a separate sheet of paper, draw a Concept Building chart like the one shown below. Write haiku in the Concept box, then read the selection. After you read, explain what haiku is in the Definition box. Write the guidelines for writing haiku in the Steps box. For this lesson, write your own haiku in the Review box.

Strategy Tip

You can vary the labels in your Concept Building chart. The third box in this chart is usually labeled *Evidence*. In this essay, the labels *Steps* or *Qualities* might be more useful.

Concept	Definition or Formula	Evidence or Steps	Review or Examples

Strategy Tip

Here's an example of a haiku. Read it carefully. It will help you understand the main concept of the essay.

The Beauty of Haiku

on a bare branch
a crow has settled
autumn dusk

The poem above is a **haiku**. It was written by Japan's master of the form, Bashō. Writing a haiku probably looks easy. After all, haiku are short. They have only three lines. They describe everyday things. However, as you will learn, writing haiku is no simple matter.

Haiku is a Japanese form of poetry. It is related to the oldest poems in Japan. These poems were composed as prayers to the gods and thanks to kings. These early poems were called *tanka*. In the 14th century, a variation of tanka was popular. By the 19th century, this form of poetry was called *haiku*.

Japanese haiku have five syllables on the first line, seven syllables on the second, and five syllables on the third line. You'll notice that the examples given here don't follow that pattern. That's because these haiku have been translated. In the original Japanese, you would see the 5–7–5 syllable pattern.

Essay:
The Beauty of Haiku

Strategy Tip

The subheadings on this page tell you how to write a haiku. You might note them in the Steps box of your Concept Building chart.

Vocabulary Tip

You can figure out the meaning of *judgmental* by using a word you do know: *judge*. What does it mean to *judge* someone? It means "to express an opinion" about that person.

Vocabulary Tip

The meaning of *evoke* does not appear right after the word. Clues to its meaning are in the paragraph, though. What clues can you find to help you define *evoke*?

The syllable count isn't the only thing that's special to haiku. As you think about haiku, keep the following guidelines in mind.

Don't Create Sentences

Look at the haiku at the beginning of this article. The writer has created images, not sentences. Haiku sound more like thoughts than conversation.

Use Images from Life

One reason haiku are so powerful is that they are not about ideas. The poet doesn't tell the reader what to think or feel. The poet refers to concrete, or clear, images the reader can *experience*. He or she can taste, smell, touch, or feel. In a great haiku, the reader experiences a vivid image in every line. Here is an example:

> such stillness
> the shrill of a cicada
> pierces rock

Avoid Judgmental Adjectives and Adverbs

Some adjectives can make an image clear. A *yellow* flower and an *icy* rain are concrete images. Other words, though, show a judgment—a *beautiful* flower. The word *beautiful* tells the reader what to think. Haiku just describe. The thinking is left to the reader.

Create Two or Three Clear Images

Don't overload the poem with many different images. Create one clear image with every line. If you can create two strong images in the poem, you're doing very well. Haiku masters often add a twist to the third image. That twist makes us see the last images in a new way. Here is one example from Bashō:

> blowing stones
> flying from the volcano Asama
> autumn gale

Understand the Feelings of the Seasons

Much of Japanese haiku is based on the feelings the seasons **evoke**. In traditional haiku, spring is the time for birth. The images are of young animals and cherry blossoms. When a seasonal reference is out of place in a haiku, that "mistake" is always intended. It creates a contrast.

Writing haiku can be a wonderful experience. The poet concentrates on using a few strokes to create a strong image. This discipline has contributed to the popularity of haiku. The images we read in the best haiku stay with us.

Apply It............ To check your understanding of the essay, circle the best answer to each question below.

1. Bashō was
    a. a famous Japanese haiku master.
    b. a well-known scholar of haiku.
    c. an American haiku master.
    d. the author of this article.

2. You can best describe the author's attitude toward haiku as
    a. respectful.
    b. disrespectful.
    c. uninterested.
    d. logical.

3. Which of these should a writer of haiku try to do?
    a. Use words that describe feelings.
    b. Create at least four strong images.
    c. Write three lines that make a sentence.
    d. Use images from life.

4. In the second paragraph from the end of the essay, *evoke* means
    a. bring to mind.
    b. imagine.
    c. pretend.
    d. forget.

5. Why does the author believe that people remember haiku?
    a. Haiku are about the seasons.
    b. Haiku give strong opinions.
    c. Haiku's strong images paint a clear picture.
    d. Haiku are very emotional.

Use the lines below to write your answers for numbers 6 and 7. You can use your Concept Building notes to help you.

6. Choose one of the haiku in this essay. Explain what it means and why you chose it.

_____

_____

Test Tip

Before you write a haiku, review the guidelines in your Steps box. Also review the essay's subheadings.

7. Write a haiku. Follow the guidelines in the article.

_____

_____

_____

Unit 2 Review
Reading in Language Arts

*I*n this unit, you have practiced using the KWL Plus, Cornell Note-taking, PACA, and Concept Building reading strategies. Choose one strategy, and use it when you read the selection below. Use a separate sheet of paper to draw charts, take notes, and summarize what you learn.

Hint *Remember that all reading strategies have activities for before, during, and after reading. To review these steps, look back at Unit 1 or at the last page of this book.*

The Broadcast that Shook the World

It was Sunday night, October 30, 1938. As they usually did, many Americans sat down by the radio and tuned in the Mercury Theater on the Air. Then they settled back, ready to enjoy a radio play. What they heard caused a national panic.

Those who tuned in at the beginning heard the announcer say they were listening to a radio play. Those who tuned in later heard dance music. But then, the play began. A nervous announcer broke in to say that astronomers had seen gas explosions on Mars.

The dance music went back on. A few minutes later, there was another bulletin. A "huge flaming object" had landed in New Jersey. Hundreds of people had been killed. The object was a space ship. Inside were strange creatures from Mars.

It's Wriggling out of the Shadow!
The announcer was breathless. "Good heavens, something's wriggling out of the shadow like a gray snake," he said. "Now it's another one, and another. They look like tentacles to me. There, I can see the thing's body—it's as large as a bear, and it glistens like wet leather. But that face! I can hardly force myself to keep looking at it. The eyes are black and gleam like a serpent. The mouth is V-shaped, and saliva is dripping from its rimless lips. The lips seem to quiver."

Later in the broadcast, the announcer said the audience was listening to a radio play. The dance music came back on, and then more "news." The Martians were attacking! They had death rays, and Earth was under fire!

Some people never heard that they were listening to a play, while others heard and paid no attention. There was widespread panic. Calls flooded police and fire stations; the New York City police sent out a message that the Mars attack was a radio play.

The broadcast only lasted an hour. At the end, the earth was "saved." The germs from Earth sickened the monsters from Mars, and they began dying in the streets of New Jersey. Some people never heard that news, either. They were in hospitals, getting treatment for panic, or they were headed far out of state.

It was hours before life got back to normal. CBS, which had broadcast the play, apologized. The play was based on H.G. Wells's novel *War of the Worlds,* the network explained.

Could This Happen Today?

Could a broadcast panic the country that way today? Probably not. There are so many sources of information that a single broadcast would never be believed.

Radio and television still have a powerful effect on people's thinking, however. People hear someone on television and assume that what the person says is correct. The *War of the Worlds* broadcast offers a powerful reminder. Be careful what you broadcast. You may be believed.

Use your notes and charts to help you answer the questions below.

1. The main idea of this selection is that
   a. Today, no one would mistake a radio play for real life.
   b. Most people believe anything that is broadcast.
   c. People listening to a radio play thought it was a news report.
   d. In 1938, people didn't realize that radios could broadcast plays.

2. Which is *not* a description of the way people reacted to the broadcast?
   a. They tried to leave New Jersey.
   b. There was widespread panic.
   c. Some people were overcome with panic and went to the hospital.
   d. They wanted to regulate radio.

3. In the radio play, what caused the death of the Martians?
   a. They were blasted by the air force.
   b. They did not die.
   c. They died from Earth germs.
   d. They died because of Earth air.

4. Why do you think so many people believed that the *War of the Worlds* was real?

_____

_____

5. Do you think radio shows like *War of the Worlds* should be broadcast? Explain.

_____

_____

_____

Unit 3
Reading in Social Studies

You already read many kinds of social studies texts both in and out of school. You read history, geography, and government textbooks in school. At home you may read newspaper stories about news events. When you plan a vacation, you may read about the weather in your destination. You also may read to learn more about where you are going. Reading in social studies is a skill you will use often.

How Social Studies Reading Is Organized

Social studies consists of several subjects. These subjects include history, geography, and civics. Within these subjects you also may read about a culture or about economics. However, there are some patterns in the ways social studies readings are organized. When you recognize these patterns, you will better understand what you read because you'll be able to predict what will come next. Here are some common social studies patterns. You may see a combination of these patterns in one selection.

Main Idea and Details. This pattern in reading focuses on one main idea. Any social studies reading may be organized in this way. An article may explain a law. A history text may discuss a battle. When you see this organization, you know several points will explain or define the main idea.

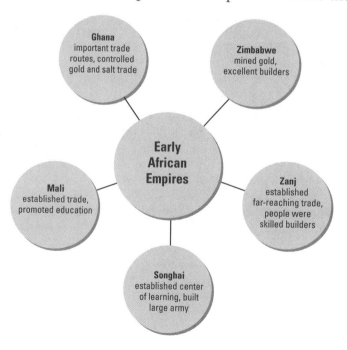

Compare and Contrast. Some reading requires you to think about how two things are alike and how they are different. For example, you may read about how two economic systems are similar. You may read about how two countries are different. When you see this pattern, you know the author wants you to think about what is alike and what is different about these topics. A Venn diagram like the one below can make the comparisons clear.

Athens and Sparta

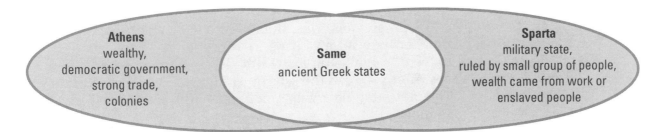

Sequence of Events. You will often see this pattern in history texts. Events are presented in chronological, or time, order. Creating a timeline or a series of boxes can help you understand and keep track of this pattern. It also can help you see how one event led to another event.

The Civil War

Getting the Most from Your Reading

If you can recognize the way a reading is organized, you will better understand what you read. You will be able to think about what kind of information might be next and how all the points in the reading fit together. Drawings like the ones on these two pages can show you these patterns. Thinking about how a reading is organized can help you understand—and remember—what you read.

Lesson 7

Economics: Teen Power

Understand It......

Hint

You can review the KWL Plus strategy on page 12.

Economics is part of everyday life. People get money and they spend it. They often spend it because advertisements have persuaded them to buy products. That's what this article is about: advertisers' efforts to attract teenagers. Because you probably know a lot about this topic, KWL Plus is a good reading strategy to help you understand the article.

What do you know about how advertisers try to influence your spending decisions? Do you believe what commercials say when you see them on TV? If a commercial has good music and good special effects, do you think the product might be good, too? If you already like a product, do you tend to trust the advertising? Do you ever try to talk your parents into buying certain brands?

Try It.............

Think about all of these questions, then draw a KWL chart like the one below on a separate sheet of paper. Write what you know about marketing to teens in the K column. In the W column, write what you want to know. After you read the selection, add what you learned to the L column. The more complete your L column is, the easier it will be to write your summary.

Strategy Tip

The K column of your KWL chart should include not just what you have read about but also what you know from your everyday life.

K (What I know)	W (What I want to know)	L (What I've learned)

Vocabulary Tip

You probably know one meaning of *target*. It can be a noun meaning "goal." Think of the meaning you know to figure out what *target* means as a verb.

Teen Power

If you think advertisers **target** younger and younger people, you're right. Advertisers have discovered that teens have a huge amount of money to spend. There is more to it than that, though. Advertisers gear their ads toward teenagers for many reasons.

First, and perhaps most important, teenagers have become a huge market. Advertisers want that market. Teens spend almost $100 billion a year. Part of what they spend is their own money. Teenage girls spend about $34 a week. Boys spend $44. Teenagers also spend their families' money. For instance, more than half of teen girls and one-third of teen boys do at least some food shopping for their families.

Trendsetting Teens

It isn't just the money teens spend that makes them important. Teens also influence what their parents buy. They may add items to the cart when shopping with their parents. They also may ask their parents to buy certain brands for them. Parents may ask their teenagers what they want or ask their advice about what to buy.

Advertisers have also learned that teens set trends. What teenagers decide is cool often becomes cool everywhere. Younger children look to teens for advice about what to buy. Here's a surprise, though: Parents also look to their teenagers to find out what is cool.

Today's teenager is tomorrow's adult. To an advertiser, that means a future market. Even if teenagers don't buy cars today, they will soon. Car companies market to the buyers of tomorrow.

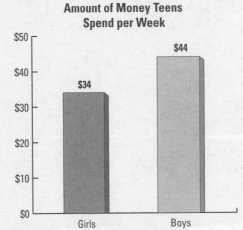

At the same time that advertisers see how important teens will be, they also see the teenage market growing. For many years, the number of teenagers decreased every year. Today, that number is growing. The children of baby boomers are becoming teenagers. By 2010, there will be 34.9 million teenagers in the United States.

What Makes Teenagers Buy?

Once advertisers decided to target the teenage market, they faced another question. What makes teenagers buy? The answer: Teens like what is cool. Researchers now had another question to answer. What makes a product cool?

Teenagers say the most important way to judge cool is quality. If a product is a quality product, it is cool. The next most important thing is a product made "for people my age." Ads themselves can make a product cool, a finding that must have made advertisers happy.

Strategy Tip
You'll often see bar graphs like this one in an economics article. Look at them carefully. They contain important information. They can also help you add questions or answers to your KWL chart.

Now that you've finished reading this article, complete the L column of your KWL chart. Look back at your W questions. Did you answer all of them? You may want to reread if you think the answers to your questions are in the article.

The last step of the KWL Plus strategy is to write a summary of what you have read. Use your KWL chart to help you. Be sure to include the main points of what you have read and details that support them.

Economics: Teen Power

Apply It . . . . To check your understanding of the article, circle the best answer to each question below.

1. The main idea of this article is that
   a. teenagers influence buying patterns for everyone.
   b. advertisers are gearing more ads toward teenagers for a number of reasons.
   c. teenagers have more money than ever to spend.
   d. teenagers influence the design of products.

Test Tip

Question 2 asks you for the meaning of *influence*. Before you choose an answer, look back at where the word is used in the article. Then substitute each of these choices to see which one makes sense in the sentence.

2. In the first paragraph of "Trendsetting Teens," *influence* means
   a. political power.
   b. authority.
   c. to have an effect on a decision.
   d. disagree with.

3. Which of the following is *not* a reason advertisers target teenagers?
   a. Teenagers spend more money than any other group.
   b. Teenagers are the adult buyers of tomorrow.
   c. Teenagers affect what their families buy.
   d. Teenagers set trends.

4. A car manufacturer might target teenagers because
   a. parents ask their teenagers for advice about what to buy.
   b. teenagers are better drivers than their parents.
   c. teenagers believe advertisers more than any other group does.
   d. parents don't know much about cars.

Test Tip

If you're not sure of the answer to a question, look over the article again. The subheadings might help you find the answer.

5. One way advertisers appeal to teenagers is by
   a. advertising a product heavily.
   b. mentioning that a product is a bargain.
   c. making sure their parents do not find a product appealing.
   d. making a quality product.

Use the lines below to write your answers for numbers 6 and 7. You can use your KWL chart and your summary to help you.

6. List *three* reasons that more and more advertisers try to reach teenagers.

   _____

   _____

   _____

7. Explain what advertisers think about when they create ads designed to persuade teenagers to buy.

   _____

   _____

   _____

Lesson 8

Civics: The "Glory That Was Greece"

Understand It......

Hint
You can review the Cornell Note-taking strategy on page 8.

This civics article discusses the government of ancient Greece. You may not know much about ancient Greece. That makes the Cornell Note-taking system a good choice to help you keep track of what you read. Simply read, then take notes about main points and the evidence that supports or explains them.

Try It..............

First, preview the article. Read the first and last paragraphs and all of the topic sentences carefully. If you're wondering why a government from more than 2,000 years ago might interest you, the first paragraph tells you. The ancient Greeks invented the system of government that we use in the United States today. When you read the subheadings, you'll see the word *glory* a few times. What does that word tell you about the writer's opinion of ancient Greece?

After you have previewed the article, copy the Cornell Note-taking chart shown below onto a separate sheet of paper. Be sure to make your Main Points column smaller than your Evidence column. Then read the article, watching for important information. You might think about why ancient Greece is important today. When you have finished reading, fill out your Cornell chart.

Strategy Tip
The subheadings can give you some ideas about the topic and about how the article is organized.

Main Points	Evidence/Details

Vocabulary Tip
In social studies texts, terms like *city–states* are often followed by definitions.

The "Glory That Was Greece"

When people talk about ancient Greece, they often speak of the "glory that was Greece." This is because many people think that the government of ancient Greece was the first one to use democracy.

Greece's origins date back to about 1900 B.C. The early Greeks were nomadic herders. They roamed from place to place to find good pastures for their animals. Then people began to settle in one place, forming **city–states**. Each city–state had a separate government. Ancient Greece was not a unified nation. Instead, Greek citizens were loyal to the cities they lived in. These city–states were small. Athens was the only city–state with more than 20,000 residents.

Civics:
The "Glory That Was Greece"

Strategy Tip

When you see a list with words in bold type or bullets (dots), you can assume the information is important. Add this information to your Cornell chart.

The government of a city–state generally went through several stages.

- **The Age of Kings**. In early times, the ruler was a rich landowner who acted as a king. That system lasted until about the 8th and 7th centuries B.C.

- **Oligarchy** (rule of the few). Wealthy landowners who ruled together made up an oligarchy. Often, though, everyone else was unhappy. In addition, the landowners often quarreled among themselves.

- **Tyranny**. When people who were ruled by an oligarchy became very unhappy, one of the rulers would promise relief. Then he would seize power. Today, *tyrant* has a negative meaning. A tyrant is a person who rules without the permission of the people. In ancient Greece, though, a tyrant was simply a ruler who was not born into a royal family.

- **Beginnings of Democracy**. Often, a tyrant told his subjects they should have a voice in decisions. The idea became common in many city–states. The city–state of Athens led the way. By the 5th century B.C., Athens was the world's first democracy. In a democracy, lawmakers are elected by the people.

The Glories of Athens

When people speak of the wonders of ancient Greece, they usually mean Athens. Athens's rulers realized that a strong navy was the key to success. Athens controlled a large area with its ships. This meant the city–state had plenty of tax money. Athens's citizens got the benefits. The city was filled with sculpture and paintings. Education had been only for a few rich people. It soon became available to many.

However, Athens had a side that was not glorious. The miseries of enslaved people helped make the rich life possible for Athenians. Historians estimate that one-fourth to four-fifths of the people living in Athens were enslaved. Many enslaved people had been defeated in war. Others were simply captured. Some enslaved people were able to buy their freedom. Many, however, lived terrible lives.

Because the citizens of Athens had enslaved people to do their work, they had plenty of extra time. Athenians painted and wrote. People who are trying to find food to eat do not have those choices. This meant that Athenians had the time to produce remarkable ideas about philosophy and government.

In Athens, every citizen could vote, but not everyone could be a citizen. Women, enslaved people, and people from outside Athens could not be citizens. Every ten days, the Assembly of Citizens met. At least 6,000 citizens attended each meeting. If they failed to come, police rounded them up.

At the assembly, any citizen could speak. A council of 500 was chosen every year by lottery. The council chose the topics to be discussed. The council also ran the city. Citizens took turns being generals and judges.

Being a citizen in Athens had its dangers. Once a year, the Assembly handed out broken pieces of pottery. If a citizen wanted to **exile** someone, he scratched the person's name on the pottery. If more than 6,000 voters agreed, the man was **exiled** from Athens for ten years.

The End of the Glory

Envy and ambition caused the end of Athens's glory days. As Athens gained power, neighboring city–states grew angry. Finally, in 431 B.C., the struggle that ended Athens's power began. The war pitted the naval power of Athens against the land power of Sparta, another large city–state. In the first part of the war, Athens struck at its enemies from the sea, refusing to fight on land. However, a deadly plague struck Athens, killing one-fourth of its residents. One of the dead was Pericles, the leader of Athens. The city drifted like a ship without a captain.

The next leader, Alcibiades, dreamed of fame as an army leader. He began a great land attack. The Athenian army was destroyed. Its soldiers were enslaved. In 404 B.C., Athens became part of Sparta. Sparta's traditions were not as democratic as those of Athens. The glory days of ancient Greece were over.

Vocabulary Tip

Sometimes, an unfamiliar word appears more than once, as *exile* does here. By comparing the different ways the word is used in context, you can guess at its meaning.

After you have finished reading the article, note the main points and details you've found in your Cornell chart. Use these notes to write a summary of the article.

Apply It. . . . . To check your understanding of the article, circle the best answer to each question below.

1. Which of these was *not* true of the Athenian Assembly?
   a. Enslaved people were not allowed to attend.
   b. Any citizen could speak.
   c. The council was chosen by lottery.
   d. The Assembly began in Sparta.

2. Athens lost its democracy after Sparta won the war in 404 B.C. because
   a. Sparta wanted to teach Athens a lesson.
   b. all Athenians were enslaved.
   c. Sparta used its own system of government.
   d. Athenians realized that democracy had made them weak.

3. Athens's navy was important in its history because
   a. it allowed Athens to control a large area, collect taxes, and become rich.
   b. the commanders of the navy were also the city's leaders.
   c. it allowed the navy to make money for Athens through trade.
   d. the navy wanted a democracy.

4. In the first section of the article, *oligarchy* refers to
   a. a citizen of Athens.
   b. a system of government in which every citizen has a vote.
   c. a system of government in which a few people have power.
   d. the government of Sparta.

5. Athens fell because
   a. the people had become lazy from not working hard.
   b. it lost a war to Sparta.
   c. its enslaved people rebelled.
   d. the citizens did not want to fight.

Use the lines below to write your answers for numbers 6 and 7. You can use your Cornell notes and your summary to help you.

6. Think about the democracy we have in the United States today. How would you compare and contrast democracy in the United States to democracy in ancient Athens?

_____

_____

_____

Test Tip

Question 7 asks for evidence. When you give evidence, you need to write facts and details from the article.

7. Why did having a lot of spare time lead ancient Athens to develop a "glorious" civilization? Give evidence from the article to support your answer.

_____

_____

_____

Lesson 9

Geography:
The Silk Road

Understand It......

Hint
You can review the PACA strategy on page 4.

This geography selection tells about a famous trade route in Asia called the Silk Road. The PACA strategy is a good one to use with this selection because the map offers a lot of information. Use this information to make predictions about the selection.

Try It.............

Draw a PACA chart like the one below on another sheet of paper. Then preview the selection. As you preview, look at the title and the subheadings. Also look at the map. Use that information to write a few predictions in the Predictions column. Since you will be reading a geography selection, you might guess that some information will be about places or landforms. What do you predict the "Silk Road" will be?

After you read the selection, fill in your PACA chart. Remember to make a check mark next to each prediction that proved to be correct. When you see important information you did not predict, write that. Make a star next to these new points. In the Support column, write the evidence that supports or confirms each prediction. Cross out any incorrect predictions.

Strategy Tip
In a geography selection, *what* and *where* questions are important. However, ask a few *why* questions to be sure you understand the point of the reading.

Predictions	Support

Vocabulary Tip
You probably know *pass* as a verb, meaning "to go by something." Use that information to define *pass* as a noun. What might a mountain *pass* be?

The Silk Road

The mountain **passes** were terrifying. Avalanches and falling rocks were common. Most travelers avoided the great desert. At any moment, fierce bandits might strip travelers of all they owned. However, for 1,600 years, the 5,000-mile Silk Road was so important that traders risked all these dangers. The end of the road, they knew, meant wealth almost beyond measure.

The Silk Road runs between China and Europe. It became an active trade route about 100 B.C. For the first time, people in Europe and Asia could exchange goods. Most important, Europeans could transport their gold to China and bring back silk.

Europeans loved silk. The fabric reached Rome around the 1st century B.C. The Romans had no fabric as soft, as shimmering, or as fine. Almost instantly, silk became the favorite fabric of the rich. It was worth its weight in gold. The high price of Chinese silk made the dangers of the Silk Road a reasonable risk for traders.

Geography:
The Silk Road

Chinese silk makers soon realized they possessed a valuable trade secret. Silk making was almost unknown outside China. Silkworms spun cocoons. The silk makers carefully unraveled the cocoons into silken thread. They then wove the thread into silk cloth. The Chinese mastered the art of silk making.

From the Edge of Civilization

On its eastern end, the Silk Road began in Changan, the capital of the Chinese empire at the time. Today, Changan is called Sian. From Changan, caravans of camels set off for 500 miles along a fertile stretch of land to Dunhuang.

The Chinese considered Dunhuang to be the edge of civilization because, for the next 900 miles, the caravans had to cross the Tarim Basin. This basin is one of the most terrifying stretches of land on Earth. It is home to the Takla Makan, the driest desert in Asia. Sand dunes there have buried cities. Water is scarce. Travelers on the Silk Road hoped they would not have to face swirling sandstorms or terrible temperatures. These temperatures range from -4° F (-20° C) to 104° F (40° C).

At the end of Takla Makan, caravans faced the passes of the Pamir Mountains. The narrow, death-defying ledges, which are almost 15,000 feet (4,570 m) high, nearly defeated some travelers. If the height and the narrow rock trails were not bad enough, avalanches and rock slides presented constant danger.

Strategy Tip

Look carefully at the map. What prediction can you make about how difficult it might have been to travel on the Silk Road? Why do you think so?

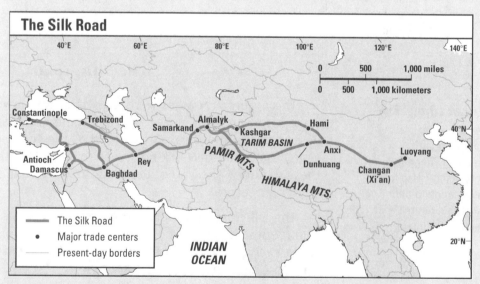

From the Pamirs, the caravans inched down to what is now Afghanistan. The traveling there became easier. The caravans took different routes. Some traveled to India. Others went to the north, through Samarkand, now called Uzbekistan. The caravans had even more choices of routes as they moved farther west.

SOCIAL STUDIES

The Adventures of Marco Polo

Perhaps the most famous traveler to **traverse** the Silk Road in ancient days was Marco Polo. He left Venice in A.D. 1271 and wrote a detailed account of his 5,600-mile (9,010 km) journey. The trip took three years. Eventually, Marco Polo, his father, and his uncle arrived in China. Marco Polo wrote of the wealth he found there. There was marble and gold. Paintings and statues were everywhere. The book they wrote about those years became one of the most well-read books of the time. However, few people believed the tales of Polo's adventures in China.

The glories of the Silk Road dimmed in the 1400s. The rise and fall of governments made the route unsafe. In addition, sailors found a passage from Europe to China that made the hazards of the Silk Road unnecessary.

The Silk Road remains an important part of world history because it connected the cultures of Europe and Asia. This connection fostered an exchange of ideas, of goods, of people, and of languages. The Silk Road marked the beginning of understanding between the two continents.

Vocabulary Tip

You can use content clues to decode *traverse*. The traveler Marco Polo *traversed* the Silk Road. He wrote about his *journey*. The *trip* took three years. These words tell you that to *traverse* the Silk Road means to "go across" it.

Look over your PACA notes. Do you need to add any major points or any supporting information? If so, add them to the Predictions column. Then add a star to the small box. When you finish, you should have a good understanding of the selection you just read.

Apply It........... To check your understanding of the selection, circle the best answer to each question below.

1. Which of these statements is *not* true?
   a. The Silk Road was an active trade route for about 1,600 years.
   b. Marco Polo's book about China was popular in Europe when it was published.
   c. Takla Makan is a terrifying mountain range.
   d. Silk was worth its weight in gold in ancient Rome.

Test Tip

Question 2 asks you to *predict* an answer. You predict an answer in the same way that you predict what you will read. Think about what you know and what you can find out. Then make a reasonable guess at an answer.

2. You might predict that if Europeans had known the secret of silk making,
   a. China would have been even more popular as the source of silkworms.
   b. fewer traders would have made the dangerous journey on the Silk Road.
   c. the Silk Road's popularity would have stayed the same.
   d. silk would have been less desired in Rome.

3. The word *fostered* in the last paragraph means
   a. helped bring about.
   b. stopped.
   c. pictured.
   d. delayed.

Geography:
The Silk Road

4. Which of these locations is closest to the western end of the Silk Road?
   a. Afghanistan
   b. Changan
   c. the Pamir Mountains
   d. the Takla Makan desert

Test Tip

Notice that each of the answers in question 5 contains two parts. *Both* parts must be correct for the answer to be correct.

5. Fewer people traveled the Silk Road in the 1400s because
   a. the route was unsafe and silk was no longer in demand.
   b. silk was less popular and the route was more dangerous.
   c. the route was unsafe and more dangerous.
   d. the route was unsafe and sailors had found an ocean passage from China to Europe.

Use the lines below to write your answers for numbers 6 and 7. Use your PACA chart and the map to help you.

6. Write a description of the Silk Road, including the major stops on the route.

_____

_____

_____

_____

7. How do you think trade might help cultures understand one another?

_____

_____

_____

_____

World History:
Lesson 10   The Battle of Belleau Wood

Understand It......

Hint

You can review the Concept Building strategy on page 16.

This world history article discusses one battle—Belleau Wood—which was fought during World War I. Because the article presents a single event or concept, the Concept Building strategy will work well to help you understand the battle and its importance.

Try It..............

When you preview the article, you'll see that the first paragraph is especially important. One sentence shows the main idea about Belleau Wood. Try this when you preview: Read the first and last paragraphs first. Then read the title, subheadings, and topic sentences.

Make a copy of the Concept Building chart below on a separate sheet of paper. Write the concept (Belleau Wood) in the first box. After you read, write a brief description of the battle in the second box. In the third box, write the details that explain the battle's importance. When you have finished filling out the chart, review what you've learned by writing a summary paragraph in the last box.

Strategy Tip

You might want to change the name of the third box in the chart from *Evidence* or *Steps* to *Explanation* for this article.

Concept	Definition or Formula	Evidence or Steps	Review or Examples

The Battle of Belleau Wood

It was June of 1918. World War I was raging in Europe. The Allies (Russian, French, and English troops) had been fighting Germany for four years. U.S. troops had recently entered the war. How could they help their exhausted allies? The Battle of Belleau Wood was important for what it showed about the U.S. troops—to themselves, to their allies in Europe, and to the Germans.

Belleau Wood is a small area in northern France. It was near a highway that led to Paris. The army that controlled the area controlled the highway. Germany had taken it, and the Allies wanted it back.

Strategy Tip

What main points in the first paragraph explain the concept of the reading? Write them in the Definition box.

A Test for the United States
The battle was critical for the United States. The French commander wanted U.S. soldiers to take the places of Allied soldiers who had died. The U.S. commander, General John Pershing, opposed that idea. He wanted his men to fight under a U.S. commander. At Belleau Wood, the United States had a chance to prove its fighting ability. General Pershing

World History:
The Battle of Belleau Wood

wanted to prove his soldiers were more than just fill-ins for the dead and wounded.

The U.S. troops went into a situation deadly enough to frighten any experienced soldier. As they entered the forest, U.S. soldiers met exhausted French soldiers who were leaving. One U.S. soldier wrote, "They looked at us like we were mad. We were walking into a **sector** that they had given up as lost. The French kept motioning with their hands, go back, go back." Fresh and eager to show their abilities, the U.S. troops had no thought of retreating. They had reached their proving ground.

The Germans had a great advantage. Belleau Wood was only one mile square. Huge boulders were everywhere. These boulders and the wood's thick trees gave the German machine guns excellent cover. In addition, the Germans had had plenty of time to hide themselves.

The Terrible Battle

The battle began on June 6, 1918. U.S. troops experienced heavy losses. They went into the wood and died one after another as the German machine gunners mowed them down. "They leaped forward and fell in droves," one historian wrote. The soldiers pressed on. For 20 days, the battle raged. Guns roared 24 hours a day. Water was scarce, and there was no chance to cook food. The U.S. soldiers ate raw bacon and potatoes they dug from the ground.

Slowly, yard by yard, the U.S. troops gained ground. They crawled over the bodies of their dead friends. They faced machine-gun fire again and again. On June 20, the United States took the wood.

However, the victory was **bittersweet**. More than half of the U.S. soldiers sent into Belleau Wood—1,087 soldiers—had been killed or badly injured. Was it worth it? Some said no. The tiny wood had cost too many lives.

Others, though, looked at what the victory meant to both sides. The Europeans no longer had any doubt about the ability of the U.S. troops. They had no doubt about their spirit, either. U.S. soldiers were ready to fight.

If the U.S. determination impressed the Allies, it terrified the Germans. One German soldier commented that U.S. soldiers were "crazy fellows, who fight like devils."

In war, attitude can matter. So can appearances. When U.S. troops went into Belleau Wood, they proved they were willing to take huge risks—and huge losses—to win. This gave new strength to their European allies. Just as important, U.S. soldiers made the Germans afraid. In war, feelings do count. One French officer said, "You Americans are our hope, our strength, our life."

Vocabulary Tip

The word *sector* may remind you of another word you know: *section*. Use this clue to help you define *sector*.

Vocabulary Tip

The word *bittersweet* is a compound word. It is made up of two smaller words. What are those words? How do the words work together to make another word?

After you read, complete your Concept Building chart. Do your notes describe the battle of Belleau Wood and explain why it was important? If you need to, go back and add a few details to complete your chart. In the last box, write a summary of what the battle was and why it was important in World War I.

Apply It. . . . . To check your understanding of the article, circle the best answer to each question below.

1. The location of Belleau Wood was important because
   a. it was near a highway to Paris.
   b. it was where the Germans had a supply of machine guns.
   c. it was close to a German supply house.
   d. it was where the Allies defended Paris against the Germans.

2. The Battle of Belleau Wood was a turning point in the war, because
   a. it proved that German troops could fight as well as U.S. troops.
   b. no one had expected U.S. troops to come into the war.
   c. the win gave new strength to the Allies and scared the Germans.
   d. the French soldiers were tired of fighting.

3. The phrase *proving ground* in the fourth paragraph means
   a. the place where U.S. troops could show they could fight.
   b. a bloody battle site.
   c. a place that hid German machine guns.
   d. the place where the most Allied soldiers died.

4. In the fourth paragraph from the end, the phrase *victory was bittersweet* means
   a. the United States won.
   b. although the United States fought hard, it lost the battle.
   c. the Germans soon retook Belleau Wood.
   d. although the United States won, a large number of U.S. soldiers died.

Use the lines below to write your answers for numbers 5 and 6. Use your Concept Building chart to help you.

Test Tip

Question 5 asks you to compare and contrast the two sides. When you *compare*, you look for similarities. When you *contrast*, you look for differences.

5. Compare and contrast the two sides in the battle of Belleau Wood. What advantages did each side have?

_____

_____

6. What do you think was the most important effect of the Battle of Belleau Wood? Support your answer with details from the article.

_____

_____

U.S. History:
Lesson 11   Tragedy at Kent State

Understand It......

Hint

You can review the PACA strategy on page 4.

During the mid-1960s and early 1970s, students demonstrated against U.S. involvement in the Vietnam War. Use what you know about the protests and the information you see when you preview as you read. The PACA strategy can also help you understand this article.

Try It..............

First, preview the article. Then, on a separate sheet of paper, draw a PACA chart like the one shown below. Write some predictions in the Predictions column. After you read, put check marks next to the predictions that you confirm. Add and star information you did not predict. Add the information that supports your predictions in the Support column.

Strategy Tip

Look at the title and the subheadings. What questions do they raise in your mind? *How* and *why* questions are especially important to ask about this article.

Predictions	Support

Vocabulary Tip

Antiwar begins with the prefix *anti-*, which means "against." So *antiwar* means "against war." Both *distrusted* and *disliked* begin with the prefix *dis-*, which means "not." So *distrusted* means "not trusted" and *disliked* means "not liked."

Tragedy at Kent State

When members of the Ohio National Guard shot four college students at Kent State University, in Kent, Ohio, the country went into shock. The **antiwar** protests against U.S. involvement in the Vietnam War had been bitter. Those who believed in the war **distrusted** and **disliked** the protesters. However, most people opposed the killings.

Beginnings of the Protests
The United States officially became involved in the Vietnam War in 1964. The U.S. government feared that the Communists fighting a civil war in Vietnam would win. Officials felt that would lead to more communism in Southeast Asia. Gradually, U.S. troops entered the fight. By 1965, President Lyndon Johnson was ordering large numbers of U.S. soldiers to Vietnam. By late 1968, student protests had become common.

The Events in May
Antiwar protests at Kent State began after President Richard Nixon announced, on April 30, 1970, that the war was expanding. Activists hit the streets May 1. That evening, violence broke out near Kent State. Police broke up the trouble. The mayor of Kent declared a state of emergency. The governor sent in the Ohio National Guard. (The National Guard in each state keeps order in emergencies.)

On the next night, May 2, more than 1,000 students gathered to protest. The ROTC building, where students trained for military service, was set on fire. Within hours, 900 national guard troops moved onto the campus.

The next day was Sunday. Guards armed with tear gas and rifles stood on the campus. Fearing violence, they ordered an end to a student rally. When some students refused to leave, some guards fired tear gas into the crowd.

At noon on Monday, May 4, about 2,000 people had gathered in the center of campus to take part in a protest. A university police officer with three guards ordered the crowd to break up. The students threw rocks. The guards answered with tear gas.

At that point, many students left. Others kept shouting at the guards. Then, about 100 guards formed a line. The students retreated behind a building. The guards who followed found themselves facing a fence. Students started throwing rocks.

Moments later, about 28 guards turned toward the students. Most of the students were less than 100 yards away. The guards began shooting. The gunfire lasted about 13 seconds. Some soldiers shot into the air. Others aimed at the students.

The students screamed and scattered. Thirteen students fell to the ground. Four were dead. Among the students, shock turned to anger. More than 200 refused to leave the area. The president of the university ordered the school to be closed.

Four students were killed when National Guard troops fired at antiwar demonstrators at Kent State University.

Across the nation, more than 200 colleges shut down. However, not everyone agreed about the shootings. Some blamed the guards. Others blamed the students.

After the Tragedy

People disagreed about who was at fault for the killings. A presidential commission reported that the shootings were not necessary. An Ohio grand jury found the guards not guilty. Charges were dropped against 24 students and a professor for inciting a riot.

Twenty years after the deaths at Kent State, the university built a memorial. On a plaque nearby are the names of the dead and injured students. Near the memorial, 58,175 daffodils bloom every spring. They represent the 58,175 American soldiers who died in Vietnam.

Strategy Tip

What does this photograph tell you about the Kent State protests and killings? Use this information to make predictions on your PACA chart.

U.S. History: Tragedy at Kent State

After you finish reading the selection, review your PACA chart. Write check marks in the small box of predictions that were correct. Add main points that you did not predict to the Predictions column. Then add a star to the small box. Be sure that you add information to the Support column.

Apply It............ To check your understanding of the article, circle the best answer to each question below.

1. The main idea of this article is
   a. to tell why the Vietnam War divided the people of the United States.
   b. to show that the National Guard was to blame for the deaths at Kent State.
   c. to argue that no one was to blame for the deaths at Kent State.
   d. to explain what happened when the students were killed at Kent State.

2. Just before the National Guard fired on the students,
   a. the guards warned they would shoot.
   b. the students threw rocks at the guards.
   c. the president of Kent State tried to calm the situation.
   d. the students yelled at the guards.

3. In the second paragraph from the end, *inciting* means
   a. setting on fire.
   b. ending.
   c. being involved with.
   d. causing.

4. The protests against the Vietnam War grew stronger when
   a. the draft of students began.
   b. the students felt they were succeeding in stopping the war.
   c. President Nixon expanded the war.
   d. the National Guard was sent in.

Use the lines below to write your answers for numbers 5 and 6. You can use your PACA chart to help you.

5. Summarize the events at Kent State that led to the shootings.

_____

_____

_____

Test Tip

When you look for *bias*, you look for words that try to persuade the reader to agree with the writer's opinion. If a reading is *biased*, it favors one side over the other.

6. Do you think the writer of this piece showed *bias*? Give examples from the article to support your answer.

_____

_____

_____

Lesson 12

U.S. History: Hell's Kitchen

Understand It......

Hint

You can review the Cornell Note-taking strategy on page 8.

This selection gives you some information about the lives of immigrants who settled in one New York City neighborhood: Hell's Kitchen. Because the topic might be new to you, it's best to use a strategy that does not rely on what you know. Try the Cornell Note-taking method to help you understand this selection.

Try It.............

Start by previewing the selection to get an idea of what you will be reading about. Think about the title and the subheadings. On a separate sheet of paper, draw a Cornell Note-taking chart like the one below. After you read, write the main points you found in the Main Points column. Write the details that support these main points in the Evidence or Details column.

Main Points	Evidence/Details

Strategy Tip

Immigrants, which you will see in the first sentence, might be your first main point. In the Evidence/Details column, you might add details about *why* immigrants lived there and *how* they lived.

Hell's Kitchen

New York City was the first place many immigrants saw when they reached the United States. It is not surprising that many stayed there. Hell's Kitchen is a neighborhood in the middle of Manhattan, a part of New York City. This history of Hell's Kitchen tells the story of some of these immigrants.

There are many theories about how this area of New York City got its nickname. Some say it was because the area was so poor and there was so much violence. Others point out that the nickname was 19th-century slang for any poor area. Still others think one of the tenement houses was given the name. It stuck to the entire area because it fit.

Of course, bad conditions were common for immigrant groups wherever they settled in the large cities of the United States. Often, immigrants arrived with little money and few ideas about how to get work. They understood little about their new country, and many spoke little English. They had few choices of jobs. They also knew few people.

That explains why so many immigrants stayed together and settled in the poorest neighborhoods. A neighborhood might be filthy and overcrowded. It might be dangerous. However, people spoke the same language and followed the same customs. Newcomers could even find some foods from home.

U.S. History:
Hell's Kitchen

Strategy Tip

When you see a new subheading, you might want to add a main point to your Cornell chart.

From Flowers to Filth

According to *Virgil: The Guide to Hell's Kitchen,* this is a brief history of Hell's Kitchen and its residents. In 1803, the very wealthy businessman John Jacob Astor bought the area. At the time, it was a farm called the "Vale of Flowers." In 1803, that name fit.

In 1854, the first school was built there. It was a quiet country school. The country ways were beginning to fade, however, as New York City grew northward. By the 1860s, there was nothing left of the Vale of Flowers.

After the Dutch farmers left, the next immigrants to settle in the area were Irish and German. They lived in crowded tenement buildings. The living conditions in these tenements were terrible. A state legislature report in 1864 noted that the cattle in the neighborhood lived better than the people did. Lawmakers passed regulations requiring at least one outdoor or indoor toilet for every 20 tenants.

In the early 1860s, the Tenth Avenue Gang ruled. It joined with the Hell's Kitchen Gang in 1868. This violent gang specialized in mugging and robbery. Gang members also demanded **protection money** from local stores.

Vocabulary Tip

Even though you may not know the term *protection money,* you can figure out its meaning. Look at the individual words. Then look at the way they appear in the sentence.

In the 1870s, social activists in New York City began to clean up Hell's Kitchen. An 1881 article in the *The New York Times* listed the problems of the neighborhood. It was filthy. Rats ruled. Smells from the slaughterhouses sickened visitors. The people wore rags. The apartments were small, crowded, and had no heat. Most did not have indoor plumbing.

However, as each immigrant group found its way in the United States, many people in the group moved on. They gained enough knowledge and money to leave the area. They wanted better places to live and better schools.

Italians moved in during the 1920s. Then came Greeks and Poles. Other Eastern Europeans arrived. After World War II, new groups arrived. Puerto Ricans came. African Americans from the South moved to the cities. Many who came to New York City found shelter in Hell's Kitchen.

Hell's Kitchen Changes Again

By the 1950s, the area began to change again. Tenements were torn down. Even so, much of the immigrant **flavor** remained into the 1960s. Lorenzo Carcaterra, author of *Sleepers,* described the Hell's Kitchen of those days as still poor. "It was an area populated by an uneasy blend of Irish, Italian, Puerto Rican, and Eastern European laborers, hard men living hard lives, often by their own design."

Vocabulary Tip

The word *flavor* is used here in an unusual way. Use what you know about the word to figure out its meaning in this paragraph.

In the 1980s, rents rose sharply in New York City. Suddenly, Hell's Kitchen became an affordable place for young professionals to live. Today, some of the first residents remain, mixing with the newcomers. The Hell's Kitchen of gangs and hard living is largely a thing of the past, but its history remains as a short course in immigrant life.

Review your Cornell notes before you answer the questions below. Do your notes give you a clear picture of the selection? If not, reread the first and last paragraphs and the topic sentences. Add new main points and the evidence to support them. Then write a short summary of the selection to help you fix its meaning in your mind.

Apply It. . . . . To check your understanding of the selection, circle the best answer to each question below.

1. According to the selection, which of these is *not* a possible reason for the name Hell's Kitchen?
   a. The name came from a newspaper account.
   b. The name was 19th-century slang for any poor area.
   c. The area was so poor that the name seemed to fit.
   d. It was the name of a tenement house in the area.

Test Tip

When a test question asks for the main idea, more than one answer may have correct information. Only one answer, though, is the selection's *main idea.*

2. The main idea of the article is that
   a. poor people lived in Hell's Kitchen.
   b. the history of Hell's Kitchen tells part of the history of immigration.
   c. there should be better laws about the conditions people live in.
   d. immigrant groups were forced to live in Hell's Kitchen.

3. You can conclude that the immigrants who lived in Hell's Kitchen
   a. had few other choices.
   b. lived better in the United States than they had in their home countries.
   c. fought each other constantly.
   d. did not plan to stay in the United States.

4. How did Hell's Kitchen change in the 1980s?
   a. Rents rose in New York City, making Hell's Kitchen affordable.
   b. Bus service helped immigrants find jobs in other areas.
   c. New immigrants went to the West Coast.
   d. There were no jobs for immigrants.

Use the lines below to write your answers for numbers 5 and 6. Use your Cornell chart and summary to help you.

5. Why did Hell's Kitchen attract so many immigrants?

_____

_____

6. Why is Hell's Kitchen called "a short course in immigrant life"?

_____

_____

Unit 3 Review
Reading in Social Studies

*I*n this unit, you have practiced using the KWL Plus, Cornell Note-taking, PACA, and Concept Building reading strategies. Choose one strategy, and use it when you read the selection below. Use a separate sheet of paper to draw charts, take notes, and summarize what you learn.

Hint *Remember that all reading strategies have activities for before, during, and after reading. To review these steps, look back at Unit 1 or at the last page of this book.*

Mapping North America

The first maps of North America were those made by Native Americans. These maps were made on bone, on bark, on wood, and on rock.

The maps had different purposes than those of the explorers. Native Americans' maps were made for local use. They showed the locations of wars or where ancient groups had lived. Other maps showed the routes between villages. Maps might also show where family groups lived or where holy places were.

Many of the first large-scale maps of North America were made by explorers. They wanted to direct others to North America. They also wanted to show where they had been.

The First Maps of the Americas
The first known map by an outsider is from 1425. It is a Danish map that shows Greenland, which is off the eastern coast of North America. The map shows Greenland as part of Europe.

Maps of the Americas began to appear around the time of Christopher Columbus, in 1492. In some of these maps, North and South America are divided by a large ocean. In others, a river travels across Canada and connects the Pacific and Atlantic Oceans.

Another of the continuing errors in mapmaking came from one repeated mistake. In map after map, California is shown as a huge island. It took a 1747 statement by the King of Spain that California was *not* an island to clear up that confusion.

When countries began to establish colonies, maps of another sort began to appear. These maps showed where the colonies were. That was important for supply ships.

In the 18th century, France and Britain needed maps for military use. They were fighting each other in the colonies. Then the British wanted good maps to use in the war against the colonists.

Mapping the West
Those living in America began making their own maps for the war. They also made maps of their

settlements. In the 19th century, mapmakers mapped the West.

When the 1800s began, there was little knowledge of the middle of the country. There were settlements in the West, and the East was fairly well mapped. The center, though, was known only by Native Americans. One explorer reported that the middle of the country was nothing but desert.

Another push to map the West came with the railroads. To lay tracks to cross the country, railroad companies needed good maps.

By the early 1900s, North America was fully mapped. However, there are still surprises. Even in the 1980s, remote sensors on satellites were finding tiny islands in the Canadian Arctic.

Use your notes and charts to help you answer the questions below.

1. Native American maps differed from the maps of explorers because
   a. Native Americans needed maps for different reasons.
   b. Native Americans did not understand the purpose of maps.
   c. Europeans did not know much about maps.
   d. both b and c

2. Europeans used North American maps in the 18th century to
   a. mark a country's boundaries.
   b. plan battles.
   c. help explorers reach America.
   d. help trappers find animals.

3. Which is a reason the West was mapped?
   a. to find a route for the Revolutionary Army
   b. to find the best place to put railroad tracks
   c. to help the Europeans fight the Native Americans
   d. to find new sources of gold

4. Summarize the important points of this article.

   _____

   _____

5. What might be the effects of believing an error in a map, such as that the American West was only desert?

   _____

   _____

Unit 4
Reading in Science

You do more science reading than you think. When you read a story in the newspaper about how the weather is changing, you are reading science. When you follow the instructions for setting a VCR, you are using science reading skills. The skills you learn in reading science can help you not just in class, but in everyday life.

How Science Reading Is Organized

Much of science reading is based on adding to the knowledge you already have. You need to understand one idea before you move on to the next one. For example, you need to understand cells before you can understand the different types of cells. That process of building ideas makes reading science a careful business. You can't skip words you don't understand. Often you can't figure out a word's meaning from context. To get the most out of science reading, you need to concentrate. Knowing the way the text is organized can help. When you recognize the pattern of the text, you can fit the facts you learn into a larger picture. Here are some text patterns you may see in science reading.

Text with Diagrams. Some parts of science readings do not appear in paragraph form. Instead, the reading will be in the form of words in or near a diagram or illustration. Even though diagrams have few words, you should read them slowly and carefully. Diagrams often show an object or a process that is described in the text.

Budding in Yeast

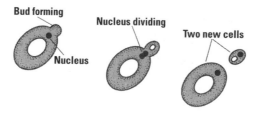

Bud forming

Nucleus dividing

Two new cells

Nucleus

Cause and Effect. Science reading often shows a series of causes and effects. You may read about the forces of nature that cause waves. You may also read about causes and effects having to do with humans. When humans take actions, they can affect the earth and other living things. When you see a cause-and-effect pattern like the one on page 69, you may want to create a diagram to help you understand the reading.

How Stars Are Formed

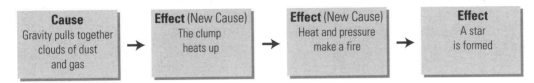

Main Idea and Details. This pattern is common in all science reading. It explains an idea or process. For example, a physical science text may discuss the types of simple machines. A life science text may describe how a cell works. Recognizing this type of organization may help you understand how all of the pieces of a reading fit together.

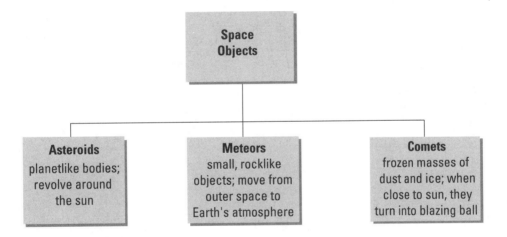

Getting the Most from Your Reading

If you can recognize the way a reading is organized, you will better understand what you read. You will be able to think about what kind of information might be next and how all the points in the reading fit together. Drawings like the ones on these two pages can show you these patterns. Thinking about how a reading is organized can help you understand—and remember—what you read.

Life Science:
Lesson 13 Medicinal Uses of Leeches

Understand It...... Modern medicine has changed a great deal over the years. Or has it? In this selection, you will learn about a medical treatment used hundreds of years ago. You'll also discover that doctors of today recognize its value.

Hint
You can review the Cornell Note-taking strategy on page 8.

Because this subject might be new to you, using the Cornell Note-taking system can help you find the selection's main points and details. You will then use this information to summarize the selection.

Try It............ Look at the illustration and read the first and last paragraphs and the topic sentences of the selection. Also read the title and subheadings. This preview will give you an idea of what you will read about. Next, copy the chart shown below onto another sheet of paper. After you read, list key words or ideas in the Main Points section of your chart. List details that support or explain these words and ideas in the Evidence or Details section. You will use this information to write your summary.

Strategy Tip
The subheadings of science selections often signal a new main idea. Add them to the Main Points section of your Cornell chart.

Main Points	Evidence/Details

Medicinal Uses of Leeches

Leeches are flat-bodied worms. They live in damp, watery environments, such as shallow rivers or lakes. A leech's body, which can be as long as 8 inches, consists of many segments. At each end of its body is a sucker. The front sucker acts as a mouth. The leech uses the rear sucker to move.

What Leeches Do

Some species of leeches eat dead plants and animals. Other species feed on living organisms. Leeches attach themselves to organisms with the front sucker. They use razor-sharp teeth to make a wound. Then they suck blood and tissue from the living host. The leeches' unique way of feeding earned them the name "bloodsuckers."

One type of bloodsucking leech releases certain chemicals as it makes a wound. One of these chemicals stops the living host's blood from thickening, which makes drawing blood easier for the leech. Another chemical acts as a painkiller. That reduces the host's **discomfort.**

Vocabulary Tip
The prefix *dis-* means "not" or "lack of." How does this prefix change the meaning of the root word *comfort*?

Leeches in Medical History

In the 18th century, doctors used leeches to treat illnesses. They thought bad blood caused disease. They believed that ridding a patient of bad blood would cure an illness. Doctors applied bloodsucking leeches to patients' bodies to remove this bad blood. "Bleeding" was a common treatment for most ailments.

A woman bleeds herself using leeches. A large glass container of leeches sits near the woman.

Leeches Today

Today, doctors know much more about the human body. They understand that bleeding a patient often causes more harm than good. They recognize that bleeding weakens patients and increases the possibility of infection. So why has the medicinal use of leeches recently increased?

Modern physicians have discovered that bloodsuckers can sometimes help the healing process. A leech can remove excess blood from an injured area to reduce swelling. Less swelling means less discomfort for the patient. Doctors sometimes use leeches to treat bruises and black eyes.

Leeches can also help trigger blood circulation. Poor circulation is a problem for patients who undergo surgery to reconnect a body part. In one **reconstructive** operation, doctors reattached a patient's thumb. However, the area was so swollen that blood could not flow into the thumb. Leeches drew out the excess blood. The swelling went down, circulation improved, and the patient regained the use of the thumb.

Not all of the medical "cures" of the past are coming back into style. Doctors are giving some older treatments a new look to see why—and if—they can work in the 21st century. In some situations, the old treatments may be the best choice. Today, though, doctors usually combine them with modern ideas and understandings to get the best of both worlds—and to help heal their patients.

After you finish reading the selection, create your Cornell chart. Make sure the details you list fully explain your main points. Use your notes to write a summary of the selection. Be sure to include all of the main points you noted and the details that support them.

Life Science:
Medicinal Uses of Leeches

Apply It. . . . . To check your understanding of the selection, circle the best answer to each question below.

1. What is a leech?
   a. a type of insect
   b. a type of earthworm
   c. a flat-bodied worm that lives in wooded areas
   d. a flat-bodied worm that lives in water

2. In reconstructive surgery, the surgeon
   a. removes a diseased body part.
   b. repairs a damaged body system.
   c. rebuilds a damaged body part.
   d. improves the condition of the blood.

3. What did 18th-century doctors believe caused disease?
   a. bad blood
   b. germs
   c. poor eating habits
   d. lack of sleep

Test Tip

Question 4 asks you to draw a conclusion. Think about the facts you have learned in the selection. Based on what you have learned, which of these choices makes the most sense?

4. What conclusion can you draw after reading the selection?
   a. Leeches have no place in modern medicine.
   b. In special situations, leeches can help a patient.
   c. Leeches are a natural way of curing disease.
   d. In most situations, leeches help a person stay healthy.

5. Which of the following is *not* a fact?
   a. Leeches are flat-bodied worms.
   b. Leeches use suckers to attach to hosts.
   c. Leeches can be used to treat a black eye.
   d. Leeches feed on the remains of dead organisms.

Use the lines below to write your answers for numbers 6 and 7. Use your Cornell notes and summary to help you.

6. Explain how leeches can help a person who has had reconstructive surgery.

_____

_____

7. Suppose a doctor wanted to treat someone you know with leeches. Would you allow the treatment? Give reasons for your decision.

_____

_____

Lesson 14

Earth Science: Turn Garbage Into Gold

Understand It...... Think about how much garbage your family throws out each week. Multiply that by the number of families in your town. Multiply that by the number of families in your state, the country—the whole world. That's a lot of garbage.

Hint
You can review the PACA strategy on page 4.

Because you can make some predictions about the topic, the PACA strategy is a good one to use. You already know something about garbage, especially if taking the garbage out is your chore.

Try It.............. Copy the PACA chart below onto another sheet of paper. Then preview the article and make a few predictions about what you will learn. After you read, confirm or revise your predictions. Also note the details on your chart that support your predictions.

Predictions   **Support**

Strategy Tip
You might want to make your first prediction by thinking about the title. How do you think garbage could be turned into gold?

Vocabulary Tip
Both *organic* and *decomposition* are defined in this paragraph. The words between the commas give you clues to the meaning of *organic*. The sentence after *decomposition* defines that word.

Turn Garbage into Gold

How does your family get rid of garbage? You probably put it in a can outside your home. A crew on a truck comes and empties the can. The garbage disappears. You don't have to think about it anymore.

However, the garbage *didn't* disappear. It just moved to another location. Garbage crews take garbage to a dump or landfill. Every week, trucks dump hundreds of loads of garbage at landfills. Workers then cover it with dirt. The earth becomes a burial ground for garbage.

Some of the garbage breaks down in the soil. Bacteria and fungi feed on **organic**, or plant, matter. Those organisms break the matter apart. As the material breaks down, it releases nutrients. The soil absorbs the nutrients, becoming rich and healthy. The process is called **decomposition**. In decomposition, organic matter breaks down naturally. Decomposition is a cycle of the natural world.

You have probably seen the process in action and didn't even know it. Have you ever taken a walk in a deciduous forest in the fall? If so, you observed decomposition. The leaves fell from the trees. They landed on the forest floor. Bacteria and fungi fed on the leaves. The organic matter broke down. The soil absorbed the nutrients, creating richer soil.

Earth Science:
Turn Garbage into Gold

Unburied Treasure

You can use your knowledge of decomposition to turn trash into treasure by starting a compost pile. You'll create an environment that triggers decomposition. The process is simple—all you need is organic garbage. Your family has plenty of that. On average, U.S. families throw out about 1,200 pounds of organic garbage each year.

Begin by selecting an outdoor spot for composting. Choose a well-ventilated area. Bacteria and fungi need air to do their work. Then start piling up organic material, such as yard and kitchen garbage. Grass clippings and leaves are good yard scraps. Coffee grounds, fruit rinds, tea bags, and even eggshells are good kitchen scraps. Use a rake to mix the items together. Throw on a few shovelfuls of dirt and mix again.

You should keep your compost heap moist but not wet. That may require covering the pile during rainy weather or watering it during a dry spell. Turn the compost every few weeks and keep adding organic garbage. Your compost pile will give off some heat when the garbage starts breaking down.

Composting has many benefits. It reduces the amount of garbage dumped in landfills. Studies show that home composting can eliminate an average of 700 pounds of organic garbage per household per year that is put in landfills.

Composting benefits the soil in many ways. Added nutrients make soil fertile. Plants grow readily in such rich soil. The added nutrients also help the soil hold water. Plants use the water to carry out life processes. For those reasons, composting is popular among farmers.

Instead of sending your organic garbage off to be buried, throw it on a compost heap. Do your part to help take care of the planet.

Strategy Tip

When you see details that support your predictions, highlight them or note them. You can add them to your chart when you have finished reading.

Now that you've finished reading about composting, look back at your PACA chart. Put check marks in the boxes next to the predictions you made that were right. Add information you did not predict. Put stars in the boxes next to the points you did not make. Cross out predictions that were wrong. Then add information that supports each prediction.

Apply It . . . . To check your understanding of the article, circle the best answer to each question below.

1. What is the main idea of the selection?
   a. Composting is easy.
   b. Composting reduces garbage and makes the soil rich.
   c. Composting is a natural process.
   d. Composting helps farmers do their work.

2. What happens when organic matter breaks down?
   a. The numbers of bacteria increase.
   b. Nutrients are added to plant or animal remains.
   c. Plants grow.
   d. Nutrients are released.

3. When you start a compost pile, what should you do first?
   a. Choose a location.
   b. Gather plant and animal remains.
   c. Find a source of water.
   d. Find a large garbage can.

4. On average, how much organic garbage does a family throw out each year?
   a. 100 pounds
   b. 120 pounds
   c. 700 pounds
   d. 1,200 pounds

5. All of the following are types of organic garbage *except*
   a. eggshells.
   b. tea bags.
   c. coffee cups.
   d. leaves.

Use the lines below to write your answers for numbers 6 and 7. Your PACA notes can help you.

6. Your family wants to compost. Make a list of the steps you need to follow.

_____

_____

_____

7. Do you think every household should compost? Write a paragraph describing your position. Support your answer with evidence from the article.

_____

_____

_____

_____

Life Science:
Lesson 15 Put Aerobics to Work for You

Understand It......

Everyone wants to stay healthy. Keys to good health include a balanced diet, plenty of rest, and exercise. In this article, you will learn about a type of exercise called *aerobics*. You will discover how aerobic exercise helps keep your body healthy. Because you probably know a few things about exercise, the PACA strategy is probably a good choice to help you get the most out of the article.

Hint

You can review the PACA strategy on page 4.

When you preview the title and the subheadings, you'll see a pattern. This pattern will tell you how the article is organized. It also can help you form some predictions about what you will learn.

Try It...............

Below is a drawing of a PACA chart. Copy the chart onto a separate sheet of paper. Write your predictions in the Predictions box. After you read, check the points you predicted. Add points you did not predict and star them. Cross out predictions that were wrong. Write the support for your predictions in the Support box.

Strategy Tip

Before you make any predictions, preview the article. Think about the subheadings. You might predict *how* to "get ready," *how* to "get set," and *how* "to go."

Predictions	Support

Vocabulary Tip

Do you know what *brisk* means? It describes a type or way of walking. Look at the other words in the sentence for clues.

Put Aerobics to Work for You

What comes to mind when you hear the word *aerobics*? Do you think of a roomful of people jumping around to loud music? Aerobic exercise is any activity that increases your heart rate and makes you breathe faster. Jogging, swimming, biking, and **brisk** walking all can give you an aerobic workout.

Get Ready
Aerobic exercise helps your body in many ways. When you exercise, you burn calories and lose body fat. Your muscle mass increases. A toned and healthy body needs muscle tissue.

Your circulatory system works better if you exercise. Regular exercise makes your heart stronger. A strong heart forces blood through your arteries and veins faster and more efficiently. Regular exercise also cuts your risk of heart disease.

Get Set
You don't need to go to a gym or health club to exercise. You can do aerobic exercises anywhere. If you can't swim or bike near your

home, you can walk up and down a flight of stairs. You can also take a brisk walk inside a shopping mall.

To get the greatest benefit, you need to exercise three to five times a week. However, check with your doctor before you begin any exercise program. Begin slowly and build up gradually. If you try to do too much in the beginning, you could get hurt or "burn out." Try taking a daily walk around your neighborhood for the first week or so. Increase your speed and the length of your walk a little each day.

Remember to stretch before and after you exercise. Stretching keeps your muscles from cramping. If you feel any pain when exercising, don't stop suddenly. Slow down gradually and stretch.

Go!
Wearing the right clothing can make you more comfortable. This can help you exercise longer. Loose layers allow your body to sweat and get rid of body heat. You can remove the layers as you get warm.

Footwear is also important. The right footwear can help prevent injuries. A salesperson in an athletic footwear store can tell you what sneakers or shoes are best for the type of exercise you plan to enjoy.

Now that you know the basics, get up and get moving! Aerobics can help you have fun, feel better, and have a stronger and healthier body.

When you finish reading the article, look back at your PACA chart. Put check marks next to the predictions you made that were right. You can also revise or add predictions. Put stars next to points you did not predict. Be sure to fill in the Support column with evidence from the article that supports your predictions.

Apply It. . . . . To check your understanding of the article, circle the best answer to each question below.

1. Aerobic exercise is any activity that
    a. increases your heart rate and makes you lose weight.
    b. makes you breathe faster and become stronger.
    c. helps you lose weight and sleep better.
    d. increases your heart rate and makes you breathe faster.

Test Tip

Question 2 asks you about the tone of the article. You can think of *tone* as the way the author would sound if he or she were speaking to you.

2. The tone of this article is
    a. humorous.
    b. hopeful.
    c. mysterious.
    d. informative.

3. When you plan an exercise program, what should you do first?
   a. Check with your doctor.
   b. Create a stretching routine.
   c. Buy new shoes.
   d. Talk to a salesperson at a sports equipment store.

4. What kind of clothing should you wear when you do aerobic exercise?
   a. heavy clothing to keep warm
   b. light clothing to avoid overheating
   c. loose layers to get rid of body heat
   d. stretchy clothing so you can move easily

5. All of the following are types of aerobic exercise *except*
   a. walking quickly through a mall.
   b. sleeping for eight hours.
   c. jogging around a track.
   d. swimming laps in an indoor pool.

Use the lines below to write your answers for numbers 6 and 7. Use your PACA chart to help you.

6. A friend has decided to start an aerobic exercise program. Write a letter to your friend, explaining how he or she should prepare to start working out.

_____

_____

_____

_____

7. Make a list of aerobic activities that you did during the past week. List three ways you could add more aerobic exercise to your week. Discuss your findings in a paragraph.

_____

_____

_____

_____

_____

Earth Science:
Lesson 16 Weathering the Weather

SCIENCE

Understand It . . . . . .

Hint

You can review the Concept Building strategy on page 16.

In recent years, there's been much talk about El Niño. The year 1998 saw the strongest El Niño on record. Once El Niño faded, however, many forecasters began to predict a different weather pattern. In this article, you will learn about La Niña, the "little girl" who sometimes follows El Niño.

The Concept Building strategy can help you understand this article. When you preview, you'll discover that the reading focuses on two major concepts. Try using a chart that has two Concept boxes, two Definition boxes, and two Evidence or Details boxes. Making sure you understand the concept of El Niño will help you understand La Niña, too.

Try It . . . .

On a separate sheet of paper, draw a Concept Building chart like the one shown below. Then preview the selection. List the key concepts you see. After you read, define these concepts in your chart. Look for other details, too, that will help you understand El Niño and La Niña.

Strategy Tip

When you preview, you'll notice that the article focuses on El Niño and La Niña. Divide your chart in half or draw two charts. Write El Niño in one Concept box and La Niña in the other Concept box.

Concept	Definition or Formula	Evidence or Steps	Review or Examples

Concept	Definition or Formula	Evidence or Steps	Review or Examples

Weathering the Weather

El Niño

El Niño originally was the name of a warm current of water that appeared off the coast of South America every December. Weather forecasters now use the term to describe the warming of certain ocean currents. This warming affects the weather for a long time. El Niño, which is Spanish for "the child," refers to the infant Jesus Christ because the current usually begins during the Christmas season.

The El Niño of 1997–1998 was one of the longest on record. For more than 15 months, the Pacific Ocean was unusually warm. Weather patterns around the world changed. The United States was no exception. In the North Central region, winter temperatures were warmer than usual. In the Southeast and Southwest, winter temperatures were cooler than normal. The West Coast, especially California, had more winter storms than usual. Many California cities set new records for rain. Sacramento had more rainy days than any other California city—103 days of rain.

Earth Science:
Weathering the Weather

However, El Niño did have a positive **effect** on the weather. The warmth of the Pacific Ocean changed the usual patterns of the jet stream. The jet stream is a fast-moving current of air that flows west to east. It circles the globe high in the atmosphere. The warmth of the Pacific Ocean changed jet stream patterns. As a result, only one tropical storm struck land in the continental United States in 1997.

La Niña

Another current of water is called La Niña, or "the little girl." This current has the opposite effect of El Niño. During El Niño, ocean waters are warmer than usual. As El Niño fades, the waters return to their normal temperature. Then ocean temperatures can drop quickly. The waters change from warmer than normal to much cooler than normal. La Niña has begun.

Such major changes in water temperature cause equally severe changes in the winds that flow above the water. The cooler waters cause the winds to gain strength. Stronger winds **affect** rainfall and jet stream patterns. All those changes affect the weather—especially in the United States.

During La Niña, winter weather becomes more severe. The Southeast, which normally is warm in winter, becomes warmer than usual. The Northwest, which normally is cool in winter, becomes cooler than usual. Places that receive snow get more than usual. More tornadoes and hurricanes are created, and more of them strike land.

However, La Niña does not always follow El Niño. In fact, La Niñas follow El Niños only 30 to 50 percent of the time. The chart on the right compares the years that have seen El Niños and La Niñas.

Strategy Tip

The chart tells you that El Niño happens about twice as often as La Niña. You might include this information in your charts.

Scientists are trying to understand El Niño and La Niña. They want to develop ways to predict them. Being able to predict severe weather, such as floods and droughts, could save the United States billions of dollars in damage costs and save countless lives.

Occurences During the Past 50 Years

El Niño Years	La Niña Years
1951–1952	1954–1955
1953–1954	1964–1965
1957–1958	1970–1971
1963–1964	1973–1974
1965–1966	1975–1976
1969–1970	1988–1989
1972–1973	1995–1996
1976–1977	
1977–1978	
1982–1983	
1986–1987	
1991–1992	
1993–1994	
1997–1998	

When you finish reading the article, complete your Concept Building chart. Be sure you have included definitions of both concepts and details or evidence that explain these concepts. Use the last box in each chart to review the main points about each concept.

Apply It............ To check your understanding of the article, circle the best answer to each question below.

1. What is the jet stream?
   a. a path that airplanes follow in the air
   b. a fast-moving current of air that circles the globe
   c. a slow-moving river of air that circles the globe
   d. an unusual weather pattern that affects rainfall

2. According to the article, what is a benefit of El Niño?
   a. Dry areas receive more rain than usual.
   b. Ocean temperatures are warmer than normal.
   c. Fewer tropical storms strike land.
   d. Most of the United States has a mild winter.

3. Which of the following is true about La Niña?
   a. La Niña occurs more often than El Niño.
   b. La Niña stops tornadoes from happening.
   c. La Niña causes a permanent change in the weather.
   d. La Niña makes normal winter weather more severe.

Test Tip

Question 4 asks you to draw a conclusion. A *conclusion* sums up the main points of a passage.

4. What conclusion can you reach after reading the selection?
   a. La Niña always follows El Niño.
   b. Fewer than half the El Niños on record have been followed by La Niña.
   c. More than half of the El Niños on record have been followed by La Niña.
   d. The occurrence of La Niña is not related to El Niño.

Use the lines below to write your answers for numbers 5 and 6. You can use your Concept Building chart to help you.

Test Tip

Use the Definition and Evidence boxes in your Concept Building chart to help you answer question 5.

5. Compare El Niño and La Niña. How are they alike? How are they different?

_____

_____

_____

6. Write a paragraph explaining how a change in the temperature of the Pacific Ocean affects weather conditions in New York City.

_____

_____

_____

Understand It......

Hint

You can review the Cornell Note-taking strategy on page 8.

How many space missions have occurred during your lifetime? You probably can't name or even count them all. These experiences, though, are recent. In this biography, you will read about the first American to enter space, Alan Shepard. Try the Cornell Note-taking system to help you understand this story of his life and his famous journey.

First, preview the biography. Think about the title and what the word *pioneer* means. When you read the first and last paragraphs and the topic sentences, you'll probably guess that the biography is written in chronological, or time, order.

Try It..............

Next, copy the Cornell Note-taking chart shown below onto a separate sheet of paper. Fill in the chart after you read. You might want to reread to find the important dates and facts. Writing this information helps you remember what you've read.

Strategy Tip

Preview the biography for dates. They may note important events and clues to points you'll want to list on your Cornell chart.

Main Points	Evidence/Details

Alan Shepard, Space Pioneer

Vocabulary Tip

Sputnik is called the world's first *artificial* satellite. In science readings, an artificial satellite is a satellite that was made by humans. Natural satellites include moons and asteroids.

Since the earliest times, people have dreamed of traveling among the stars. That dream became a reality in 1957. In that year, the Soviet Union launched *Sputnik 1*. *Sputnik* was the world's first **artificial** satellite. Later that year, *Sputnik 2* carried a dog named Laika into orbit.

Four years later, Soviet cosmonaut Yuri Gagarin became the first human to enter space. Then, on May 5, 1961, NASA (the National Aeronautics and Space Administration) sent astronaut Alan Shepard into space. Shepard rode aboard the space capsule *Freedom 7*. The spacecraft blasted off from Cape Canaveral, Florida, and traveled 117 miles into space. Just fifteen minutes later, *Freedom 7* landed in the Atlantic Ocean. A helicopter crew lifted the astronaut from the sea. Shepard had completed his mission without a scratch.

The entire United States watched Shepard's flight. Schools closed. Workers stayed home. Millions of viewers saw the flight on television. Others traveled to Cape Canaveral. Shepard's trip marked the beginning of modern space exploration for the United States.

Shepard had prepared to be America's space pioneer for many years. He had graduated from the United States Naval Academy in Annapolis, Maryland. Toward the end of World War II, Shepard had served aboard a naval destroyer. He later became a Navy test pilot.

In 1959, Shepard joined the astronaut program. Seven men were chosen from more than 100 applicants. For two years, these men, who were called the Mercury Seven, trained hard. Shepard was asked why he wanted to be an astronaut. He said, "I'm here because it gives me a chance to serve the country . . . because it's a great personal challenge."

Alan Shepherd after his landing

After Shepard's historic trip, NASA **grounded** him. Flight surgeons discovered that Shepard had a medical condition that caused dizziness and partial hearing loss. Ten years later, Shepard recovered and again was cleared for duty.

In 1971, Shepard commanded *Apollo 14* on a nine-day flight to the moon. He became the fifth man to walk on the moon. He also became the first person to play golf in space. After landing on the moon, Shepard pulled out a golf club and some golf balls and made two quick shots. One golf ball landed in a crater. It was the first outer space "hole-in-one."

Three years after the *Apollo 14* flight, Shepard retired. He focused on a second career, this one in business. He also became president of the Astronaut Scholars Foundation. This foundation gives scholarships to young people who are interested in scientific research. On July 22, 1998, Alan Shepard died at the age of 74.

Vocabulary Tip

You probably know the noun *ground*, meaning "the earth." Here, the word is used as a verb: *grounded*. Use what you know about the noun *ground* to define the verb *grounded*.

Review your Cornell notes after you complete your chart. Do they give you a clear idea of Shepard's success? Use these notes to write a summary of the biography. The summary should include the important points you found and the details that explain them.

Apply It. . . . . To check your understanding of the biography, circle the best answer to each question below.

1. *Sputnik 1* was
    a. a dog that orbited Earth.
    b. the first NASA space capsule to enter space.
    c. the world's first artificial satellite.
    d. the first NASA spacecraft to land on the moon.

Physical Science:
Alan Shepard, Space Pioneer

2. Shepard's flight aboard *Freedom 7* was
   a. the beginning of modern space exploration by the United States.
   b. the beginning of NASA.
   c. the end of the Soviet space program.
   d. the beginning of cooperation between NASA and Soviet scientists.

3. Who were the Mercury Seven?
   a. the first seven NASA astronauts
   b. the first seven Soviet cosmonauts
   c. the first seven applicants to the NASA space program
   d. the first seven U.S. spacecrafts

4. What conclusion can you reach after reading the selection?
   a. Alan Shepard was a great U.S. scientist who wanted to serve his country.
   b. Alan Shepard was a gifted golfer who wanted to win many competitions.
   c. Alan Shepard was an experienced pilot who taught others how to fly.
   d. Alan Shepard was a brave pioneer who took pride in serving his country.

Test Tip

Question 5 asks you to arrange a list in time sequence. Look for sequence clue words, such as *first, then, after, before,* and *next.* Use the clue words to order the living things.

5. In what order did the first three living beings described in the biography travel into space?
   a. Laika, Alan Shepard, Yuri Gagarin
   b. Laika, Yuri Gagarin, Alan Shepard
   c. Alan Shepard, Yuri Gagarin, Laika
   d. Yuri Gagarin, Laika, Alan Shepard

Use the lines below to write your answers for numbers 6 and 7. You can use your Cornell notes and summary to help you.

6. Why might people think of Alan Shepard as an American pioneer?

_____

_____

_____

7. Write a letter to the postmaster general, suggesting a stamp to honor Alan Shepard. Be sure to provide reasons for your suggestion.

_____

_____

_____

Lesson 18
Lab Activity: Observing Plant Cells

Understand It......

Hint
You can review the KWL Plus strategy on page 12.

Have you ever looked at an object under a microscope? If so, you probably recall seeing details not visible to the naked eye. Such observations help you understand the parts of the object. They help you recognize traits that living things have in common. In this activity, your task is to understand the directions for observing plant cells.

Try It...............

The KWL Plus strategy can help you understand these directions. Start by copying the chart shown below onto a separate sheet of paper. Then look at the title. Write what you know about microscopes and plant cells in the K column of your chart.

Then preview the selection. List questions about things that you want to learn about in the W column. Your questions should focus on understanding how to use a microscope. When you have finished your KWL chart, you will write a summary that describes how to do the activity.

Strategy Tip
Directions for a lab investigation are divided into different sections. What *how* questions does each of these sections bring to your mind? Add them to the W column of your KWL chart.

K (What I know)	W (What I want to know)	L (What I've learned)

Vocabulary Tip
Important science terms are often set in **boldface** type when they are first used. These terms are usually followed by a definition.

Lab Activity: Observing Plant Cells

Background Information
Plants and animals are made up of cells. The cells differ in size and shape, but every plant and animal cell has three main parts. They are the nucleus, cytoplasm, and cell membrane. The **nucleus** controls the life functions of the cell. The **cytoplasm** surrounds the nucleus. Most of the cell's life functions occur in the cytoplasm. The **cell membrane** surrounds the cell. It controls the movement of materials into and out of the cell. Plant cells have other parts that animal cells don't have.

Materials

compound microscope	dropper
microscope slide	iodine
cover slip	skin from the inside of an onion
lens paper	

Vocabulary Tip
How does the meaning of *slide* as it is used here differ from the meaning of the word as it is used in baseball?

Procedure

1. Clean the microscope **slide** and cover slip with the lens paper. Be gentle so that you do not break either piece. Make sure you don't get fingerprints on them.

2. Use the dropper to place one drop of iodine on the slide.

Lab Activity:
Observing Plant Cells

3. Carefully put the piece of onion skin on the slide over the iodine.

4. Gently place the cover slip over the onion skin.

5. Place the slide on the microscope stage. Use the clips to hold the slide in place.

6. Focus the microscope. Look at the onion cells under low power first. Then look at them under high power. Try to find the different parts of the cell.

7. Sketch what you see.

Observations

1. About how many onion cells could you see in the specimen?

2. What cell parts could you identify?

Conclusions

1. How did the iodine help your investigation?

2. Suppose you viewed a skin cell from your body under the microscope. What cell parts seen in the onion cell would be missing from your skin cell?

3. Based on your observation, do plant and animal cells have more similarities than differences? Give evidence for your answer.

Strategy Tip

The sections labeled *Observations* and *Conclusions* list what the directions ask you to find out. What questions do they bring to your mind? Add these questions to the W column of your KWL chart.

Now that you have finished reading the activity, fill in the L column of your KWL chart with the information you learned. Then write a summary of the activity. Think of the summary as a way to tell someone else how to conduct this experiment. You might try checking your understanding by conducting the experiment described in this reading.

Apply It. . . . . To check your understanding of the reading, circle the best answer to each question below.

1. What are the three main parts of every plant and animal cell?
   a. nucleus, muscle, and cell wall
   b. cytoplasm, protoplasm, and nucleus
   c. nucleus, cytoplasm, and cell membrane
   d. cytoplasm, nucleus, and nerves

2. Why should you read the Materials section before you begin a lab activity?
   a. to make sure you have everything you need to do the activity
   b. to learn the purpose of the activity
   c. to predict what you will learn in the activity
   d. to see how much time you need to conduct the activity

3. What type of information is provided in the Procedure section?
   a. materials needed for the activity
   b. questions to be answered through the activity
   c. additional information about the activity
   d. steps to follow when carrying out the activity

4. What must you do immediately after placing the cover slip over the slide?
   a. Place the slide on the microscope stage.
   b. Put a drop of water on the slide.
   c. Place one drop of iodine on the cover slip.
   d. Clean the microscope slide.

Test Tip

To *infer* an answer to question 5, think about what you know about the magnifying power of a microscope. How do low and high power differ?

5. What can you infer from the instruction to look at the object under high power?
   a. Most cell parts are easy to see.
   b. Some cell parts are visible only after the object is magnified.
   c. Certain cell parts are visible only at low power.
   d. Plant cells are difficult to sketch.

Use the lines below to write your answers for numbers 6 and 7. Use your KWL chart and your summary to help you.

6. Do you think the results would be different if a drop of iodine was not added to the slide? Explain your reasoning.

_____

_____

_____

_____

7. Predict the problems that could arise if a student performed the Procedure steps out of order.

_____

_____

_____

_____

_____

Unit 4 Review
Reading in Science

*I*n this unit, you have practiced using the KWL Plus, Cornell Note-taking, PACA, and Concept Building reading strategies. Choose one strategy, and use it when you read the selection below. Use a separate sheet of paper to draw charts, take notes, and summarize what you learn.

Hint *Remember that all reading strategies have activities for before, during, and after reading. To review these steps, look back at Unit 1 or at the last page of this book.*

A Spring without Songbirds?

Across the United States, songbirds are silent. In the mid-1990s, scientists first began noticing that there seemed to be fewer songbirds spending their summers in North America. They set out to find out why and to decide if anything could be done to stop this trend.

There are more than 200 species of songbirds. Some of the most common are the thrushes, the orioles, and the warblers. Every spring they fly 600 miles north, across the Gulf of Mexico from Central and South America.

The fastest fliers, such as the thrushes, leave soon after sunset. They arrive at the Texas coast by midmorning of the next day. Their first stop is usually about 30 miles inland. If the weather has been nasty, they may drop, exhausted, on the coast. From there, the birds fly farther north. Some travel up to New York and beyond.

Since the 1960s, though, the number of songbirds making the journey has dropped drastically. Some scientists say the drop is as much as 50 percent.

The songbirds' problems begin in their habitats in South America. In the winter, many of these songbirds live in tropical rain forests. These forests are under attack from farmers and others who want to cut them down and use the land. As a result, the songbirds, as well as many other species, lose their home.

Trouble on the Way

Some of the dangers to songbirds come in the journey from South America to North America in the spring. One hazard is the sea crossing. Storms in the Caribbean Sea can kill birds. Others become exhausted during the long flight over the sea and die.

Problems caused by people are the biggest killers of songbirds. For example, birds often run into obstacles such as electrical transmission towers. They are killed by aircraft and cars. About 62 million birds a year may be killed that way.

Another problem is that as U.S. woodlands become suburbs and developments, songbirds have less and less habitat. There are fewer places for them to nest.

Loss of habitat means that predators can more easily find and feast on songbird eggs. Raccoons, crows, and black rat snakes love to raid songbird nests.

Saving the Songbirds

Is there anything we can do to save the songbirds? Some people suggest changing the way forests are managed to allow for larger undisturbed areas. That won't be easy to do, however.

People want to hike and camp in wild areas. In addition, developers and mining and logging companies want to use wild lands. All of these people would have to agree to set aside areas for songbirds.

Until this problem is solved, songbird numbers will continue to decline.

Use your notes and charts to help you answer the questions below.

1. Which of these statements is true?
   a. There are fewer songbirds today than there were in the 1960s.
   b. Songbird numbers are growing in both North and South America.
   c. The loss of habitat is more severe in South than in North America.
   d. both a and c

2. The main point of this article is that
   a. songbirds cannot be saved.
   b. increasing the number of songbirds will be difficult.
   c. songbirds face many threats in their journey across the ocean.
   d. developers and others want to find ways to save the songbirds.

3. Which statement below is true?
   a. The biggest threats to songbirds have to do with loss of habitat.
   b. People in North and South America are solving the songbirds' problems.
   c. North and South America blame each other for the loss of the songbirds.
   d. Farmers are the main threat to habitats on both continents.

4. Name two reasons the numbers of songbirds are declining.

   _____

   _____

5. What do you think could be done to help save the songbirds?

   _____

   _____

Unit 5
Reading in Mathematics

You use your ability to read and understand math every day. When you read how much a sale price is, you are reading math. When you learn how much a loan will cost, you are reading math. When you find out what your favorite player's statistics are, you are reading math. Math isn't just in textbooks. You read math in your daily life.

How Mathematics Reading Is Organized

When you read a novel, you might be able to skip a word you do not know and still understand what is happening in a scene. However, when you read math, you need to understand every word. You also must pay attention to the symbols, numbers, and equations. Like science, much of mathematics reading builds on what you already know. You have to understand one idea before you can move on to the next one. Notice the patterns in math reading. Once you do, you will be better able to understand what you read.

Text with Diagrams and Graphs. A diagram or graph often shows the main idea in some math reading. The words that go along with this diagram explain it. When you see this pattern, pay special attention to the diagram or graph. You will better understand the text if you redraw the diagram yourself and write an explanation.

Sports Clubs at Columbia School

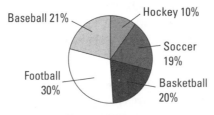

Total: 200 Members

Main Idea and Details. You will see this pattern in math reading that explains one topic. For example, you may read about the history of measurement. You may read about ways of using money. When you see this pattern, you know there will probably be one main idea and several details that explain it. The wheel-and-spoke diagram on page 91 shows this pattern.

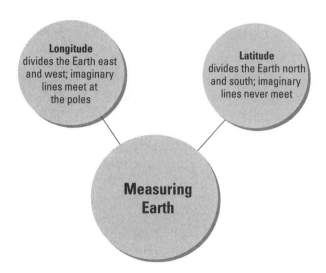

Longitude divides the Earth east and west; imaginary lines meet at the poles

Latitude divides the Earth north and south; imaginary lines never meet

Measuring Earth

Terms, Symbols, and Equations. You need to look at symbols as if they were words in math reading. A sentence in math may have only symbols. One way to understand this kind of reading is to write out the meaning of the equation. Use words to decode the symbols in the text.

$$2 \times 2 \times 2 = 2^3 = 8$$
2 times 2 times equals 4,
4 times 2 equals 8;
$$2^3 = 8$$

Getting the Most from Your Reading

If you can recognize the way a reading is organized, you will better understand what you read. You will be able to think about what kind of information might be next and how all the points in the reading fit together. Drawings like the ones on these two pages can show you these patterns. Thinking about how a reading is organized can help you understand—and remember—what you read.

Calculating Averages:
Lesson 19 Average Achievement

Understand It......

Hint

You can review the KWL Plus strategy on page 12.

Have you ever watched a baseball game? Maybe you play baseball. If so, you know that the goal of every batter is to make a base hit. Most teams keep track of the number of hits each player makes. This information is used to compute the player's batting average.

In this selection, you will learn about figuring out batting averages—and averages in general. Because you might know about batting averages, the KWL Plus strategy is a good strategy to use to help you understand the selection.

Try It..............

Draw a KWL chart like the one shown below on a separate sheet of paper. Begin by listing everything you know about batting averages in the K column. In the W column, write what you want to know about how batting averages are calculated. Think about these questions as you read the selection. When you've finished reading, you'll write the answers in the L column of your chart. Then you'll practice calculating averages.

Strategy Tip

Include what you know about how to figure out other kinds of averages in the K column of your KWL chart.

K (What I know)	W (What I want to know)	L (What I've learned)

Average Achievement

How many different kinds of averages can you think of? There are bowling averages, video game averages, and salary averages. People work an average number of hours per week. They spend an average number of hours watching TV. You have a grade-point average and sleep an average number of hours per night. You probably help with chores at home an average number of hours per week.

People figure out averages to measure overall performance. You might have **calculated** your test average. Your average gave you an idea of your overall grade. That information was useful to you. If your average was lower than you expected, you probably put in extra time studying for the next test.

Sometimes people calculate averages so they can rank things. Bowling averages might be used to rank the members of a bowling team. This information could be used to determine the order in which the team members bowl.

Vocabulary Tip

When you *calculate*, you perform a mathematical operation such as addition or subtraction. How is the word *calculator* related to *calculate*?

Baseball averages are important, too. Managers usually calculate their hitters' batting averages. A batting average is the number of hits a player gets divided by the number of times the player bats. The more hits a player gets, the higher his average is. Fewer hits per number of times at bat means a lower average.

For example, in 1995 Albert Belle went to the plate 546 times. He got a base hit 173 times. What was Belle's batting average for 1995? Divide the number of hits (173) by the number of at-bats (546). The result is .317, which was Belle's batting average.

Three years later, Belle got 200 hits. During the 1998 season, he batted 609 times. What was Belle's batting average that year? If you divide 200 by 609, you find that his average was .328. Belle's average went up.

In that same year, Mark McGwire broke a historic record. He toppled Roger Maris's record for the most home runs hit during a regular season. McGwire hit nine more than Maris did, ending the season with 70 home runs.

You might think that this many home runs would boost McGwire's batting average. In fact, his average for the season was only .299. That's because a home run counts the same as a single when calculating a batting average. McGwire had 152 hits—70 were home runs—in his 509 times at bat. Dividing 152 by 509 yields his batting average of .299.

Albert Belle

Mark McGwire

Calculating Averages:
Average Achievement

Now that you have finished reading about figuring out averages, go back and complete the L column of your KWL chart with the information you learned. Be sure you can answer every question listed in the W column.

Instead of writing a summary, practice your averaging skills by calculating the batting averages of your school's or your favorite team's baseball players. If you'd prefer, you can average the number of points per game for basketball players or the number of goals the soccer team scored during the season.

Apply It. . . . . To check your understanding of the selection, circle the best answer to each question below.

1. Why do people calculate averages?
   a. to get an idea of overall performance
   b. to rank things
   c. to practice math skills
   d. both a and b

Test Tip

The author's purpose is the reason he or she wrote the selection. Did you learn something? Did the selection cause you to take a certain stand? Did the selection make you wonder about something?

2. What is the author's purpose for writing this selection?
   a. to inform
   b. to persuade
   c. to ask a question
   d. both a and b

3. What is a batting average?
   a. the number of home runs a player hits per times at bat
   b. the number of walks a player draws plus the number of hits the player gets
   c. the number of hits a player gets per times at bat
   d. the number of times a player strikes out divided by the number of home runs

4. What information is needed to calculate a batting average?
   a. number of times at bat and number of home runs
   b. number of hits and number of times at bat
   c. number of at bats and number of strikeouts
   d. number of walks and number of hits

5. Which mathematical operation is used to figure out a batting average?
   a. division
   b. subtraction
   c. addition
   d. multiplication

Use the lines below to write your answers for numbers 6 and 7. You can use your KWL chart to help you.

6. During the regular 1998 baseball season, Bernie Williams of the New York Yankees had 169 hits in 499 times at bat. List the steps he should take to calculate his batting average.

_____

_____

_____

_____

7. Choose one activity you do every day, and figure out how much time you spend doing it. At the end of a week, calculate the average amount of time you spent each day on this activity.

_____

_____

_____

_____

_____

Lesson 20

Calculating Percentages: Tips on Tipping

Understand It......

Hint

You can review the PACA strategy on page 4.

Have you ever eaten in a restaurant that is not self-service? If you have, you probably know that you should tip the server. In this article, you will learn a method for figuring out the amount of a tip.

The PACA strategy can help you remember the main points of this article. Think about what you know about tipping. Why should people who eat in restaurants leave extra money? What should a person do if a server is rude?

Try It..............

Copy the PACA chart shown below onto another sheet of paper. Then preview the article and write some predictions about what information the article might contain. Check your predictions after you read. If you confirm a prediction, add a check mark to the small box. If you find information you did not predict, add it and write a star in the small box. You can also revise predictions. Add a star next to these predictions, too. Finally, add information to support each prediction.

Strategy Tip

The title of an article gives the reader clues about its main idea. Previewing also provides clues that help you make predictions.

Predictions	Support

Vocabulary Tip

The word *customary* is used twice in the selection. Find the sentences that contain this word. Can you think of a word you could substitute for *customary* in both sentences? Does *usual* work?

Tips on Tipping

When you eat in a restaurant in the United States, you leave a tip, or money, for your server. In some parts of the world, people do not tip their servers. Tipping is not **customary** in Japan and in many Scandinavian countries. In China, a server might consider a tip to be an insult. Waiters in New Zealand and Australia will probably refuse any tip offered. Yet, many European restaurants add a tip to the bill.

In the United States, a diner must figure out the tip. Base the amount of the tip on the cost of the meal. That does not include the sales tax. In most areas of the country, a **customary** tip is 15 percent of the bill. That amount lets the server know that the service was good. A larger tip, such as 20 percent of the meal charge, shows that the service was outstanding. A smaller tip, between 10 and 14 percent, sends the message that the service was less than satisfactory. However, a recent study showed a different result. The study found that most diners do not base their tip on the quality of service. They base their tip on the amount of the bill.

So how does a diner figure out the tip amount? First, find the total food and drink cost. That is not the final total of the bill. In many states, the final number includes sales tax. The food and drink total is shown before the sales tax is added. The tip is generally figured on the before-tax amount.

Next, decide what percentage to leave. The customer makes that decision. It should be based on the quality of service. Diners should tip fairly because tips make up a large portion of a server's wages.

Most of the time, the tip will be 15 percent. Calculate the amount by finding 10 percent of the total and then finding half of that amount, or 5 percent. Adding the two amounts yields 15 percent.

10% of total bill + 5% of total bill = 15% tip

Suppose the members of your family celebrated a birthday by eating out. At the end of your meal, you received a check for $42.50. Here is how to figure out the amount of tip.

Strategy Tip

In a math article, pay close attention to lists and examples like this one. They often show you the steps to solving a problem.

1. Find the food and drink total. It is listed before the sales tax. If your state doesn't have a sales tax, then your bill will have only one total. In this case, the food and beverage total is $42.50.

2. Decide the percentage of the tip you will leave. Because the service was satisfactory, your family decides to leave 15 percent.

3. To find 10 percent of the amount, just drop the last digit, which is 0.

4. Move the decimal point one place to the left. That yields $4.25, which is 10 percent of your total bill: $42.50.

5. Find 5 percent of the total bill. That is half of $4.25, or $2.13.

6. Add 10 percent and 5 percent to find 15 percent of the bill. In this situation, $4.25 + $2.13 = $6.38. This is the amount you should tip your server. To simplify the amount, you might want to round up to $6.50.

15% of $42.50	10% of $42.50 = $4.25 (drop last digit in $42.50)
	5% of $42.50 = $2.13 (half of $4.25)
	$4.25 (10%) + $2.13 (5%) = $6.38 (15%)

Some people use the amount of sales tax to calculate 15 percent. If the sales tax is 6 percent, doubling the tax will yield 12 percent of the food and drink total. Half of the tax will yield 3 percent of the total. If you add 12 percent and 3 percent, you will find 15 percent of the total.

In the example given above, the sales tax was 6 percent of the food and beverage total, or $2.55. Doubling that produced $5.10, which was 12 percent of the total. Half of $2.55 is $1.28, or 3 percent of the total. Adding 12 percent and 3 percent, or $5.10 and $1.28, yields $6.38. This is another way to find 15 percent of the total bill.

It does not matter what method a diner uses to calculate a tip. What is important is that the tip is fair and accurate.

Calculating Percentages:
Tips on Tipping

Now that you have finished reading about how to calculate tips using percentages, look at your PACA chart. Put check marks next to the predictions that you confirmed when reading the article. You can also revise any predictions that were wrong. Add important points that you had not thought of and mark them with stars. Remember to complete your chart by adding information that supports your predictions.

Apply It. . . . . To check your understanding of the article, circle the best answer to each question below.

Test Tip

A *fact* is a statement that can be proven to be true. Which choice given in question 1 can be proven?

1. Which of the following states a fact about tipping?
   a. It is an insult to tip a server in all countries.
   b. Tipping customs are different in different countries.
   c. Customers tip only in the United States.
   d. Tipping is not necessary.

2. A tip sends a message about the
   a. quality of service received.
   b. taste of the food served.
   c. variety of the menu.
   d. ability of the cook.

3. According to the article, many European restaurants
   a. do not allow servers to accept tips.
   b. ask that a tip be greater than the amount of sales tax.
   c. do not charge tax on meals.
   d. include a tip in the price of a meal.

4. What might a tip represent to a server in China?
   a. a compliment
   b. a raise in pay
   c. an insult
   d. a token of friendship

Use the lines below to write your answers for numbers 5 and 6. Use your PACA chart to help you.

5. In a note to a pen pal from another country, describe how to calculate a tip on a meal in a U.S. restaurant.

_____

_____

6. You have just finished a meal in a restaurant. The total bill is $13.25. That includes 6 percent sales tax of $0.75. The service you received was acceptable. How much of a tip will you leave? Explain how you calculated the tip.

_____

_____

Lesson 21

Understanding Scale: Reading a Map Scale

MATHEMATICS

Understand It...... Your family has decided to travel across the country by car. An important part of planning the trip is choosing a route. You volunteer for that job. You'll probably use maps to find the best roads to take. The maps will also help you find the shortest route. In this selection, you will learn about how to read a map, a skill you will use many times in your life.

Hint
You can review the Concept Building strategy on page 16.

Try It............... The Concept Building strategy will make it easier to understand this selection. Start by copying the Concept Building chart shown below on a sheet of paper. Then preview the selection. When you see the equations, you'll know they could help you define the concept. After you read, write a definition of map scale in the Definition or Formula box. Then write the steps for calculating a map scale in the Evidence or Steps box. Finally, check your understanding by practicing using a map scale in the Review or Examples box.

Strategy Tip
If the main concept is a formula for solving a problem, explain it in your own words. That will help you remember the formula.

Concept

Definition or Formula

Evidence or Steps

Review or Examples

Vocabulary Tip
What does *relative* mean in this reading? How does the meaning differ from the meaning of the word in the sentence "Aunt Jane is my favorite relative"?

Reading a Map Scale

A map is a flat drawing of an area. There are many different kinds of maps. You might have a map of your school attached to a notebook. A map of the United States might be displayed in your classroom. You may have used a map of a large amusement park to get to a favorite ride—or even to get to the amusement park.

Maps show the locations of places. Some maps show the **relative** positions of places. Those maps simply show that one item is north—or south, west, or east—of another. An amusement park map probably shows relative position. It would show that the roller coaster is south of the carousel or that the ice cream stand is east of the main gate.

Other maps are drawn to scale. That means that distances between places on the map represent the real distances between the places. How does a mapmaker show hundreds of miles on a small piece of paper? He or she uses a map scale.

Understanding Scale:
Reading a Map Scale

A map scale is usually at the bottom of the map. The scale is a line segment marked with numbers. The numbers show the number of miles or kilometers the segment represents.

The map scale below is from a road map. It shows that 1 inch on the map represents a distance of 20 miles. The reader can use that information to determine the actual distance between two locations on the map.

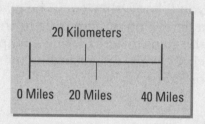

Suppose that Centerville and Maple Run are two locations on the map. The map distance between the two places is 2 inches. To find the actual distance, you write a proportion.

$$\frac{1 \text{ inch}}{20 \text{ miles}} = \frac{2 \text{ inches}}{d}$$

Strategy Tip

Take note of the examples in a math selection. They can help you understand the concept.

In this proportion, d stands for the actual distance between Centerville and Maple Run. To solve for d, multiply 20 by 2. Divide the product, 40, by 1. The result is 40. This means that the actual distance between the locations is 40 miles.

Suppose Harleytown and Elmwood are also on the map. The map distance between them is 3.5 inches. Again, you use a proportion to find the actual distance.

$$\frac{1 \text{ inch}}{20 \text{ miles}} = \frac{3.5 \text{ inches}}{d}$$

To solve for d, multiply 3.5 by 20. Divide the product, 70, by 1. The result is 70. You know that the actual distance between the locations is 70 miles.

You can use this process any time you need to find the actual distance between locations. Just make sure to check the map scale. Each map has its own scale. On a map of a small area, such as your town, 1 inch can represent 1 mile. On a map of a large area, such as your state, 1 inch can represent 50 miles. The ratio changes from map to map. However, the way you use the scale to find actual distances remains the same.

Now that you know how to use a map scale, go back and complete your Concept Building chart. Be sure to add all of the steps described in the selection. Then use that information to practice calculating a map scale in the Review or Examples box.

Apply It. . . . . To check your understanding of the selection, circle the best answer to each question below.

1. How are all maps alike?
   a. All maps have a map scale.
   b. All maps show distances in inches.
   c. All maps show the locations of places.
   d. All maps have a map scale and show distances in inches.

2. Which of the following is a true statement?
   a. A map that shows the relative positions of places is always drawn to scale.
   b. All maps show the actual distance between locations.
   c. All maps are drawn to scale.
   d. A map drawn to scale shows the actual distance between locations.

3. What information is given in a map scale?
   a. the number of towns shown on the map
   b. the number of people who live in the area
   c. the date the map was drawn
   d. the actual distance the scale represents

Test Tip

A *conclusion* is a statement that summarizes the key points of a reading. Which choice in question 4 sums up the main points of this selection?

4. What conclusion can you reach after reading the selection?
   a. Being able to use a map scale is a valuable life skill.
   b. Map scales are unnecessary.
   c. Only drivers need to know how to use a map scale.
   d. Every map should have a map scale.

5. In order to find the real distance between two places on a map, you must know
   a. how many people live in the locations.
   b. the distance a segment of the scale represents.
   c. who created the map.
   d. both a and b

Use the lines on the next page to write your answers for numbers 6 and 7. Use your Concept Building chart to help you.

Understanding Scale:
Reading a Map Scale

6. How does a map that shows relative position differ from a map that is drawn to scale?

_____

_____

_____

7. Find a map that has a scale. Choose two places shown on the map that are not too close together. Use the map scale to find the distance between these two places. Describe how you did this on the lines below.

_____

_____

_____

_____

_____

Lesson 22

Analyzing Data: Sample a Survey

MATHEMATICS

Understand It......

Hint
You can review the Cornell Note-taking strategy on page 8.

Have you ever been stopped in a mall or contacted by telephone and asked to give your opinion about something? If you have, you took part in a survey. Surveys are a common way of finding out what people like and dislike. Businesses use that information to plan new products or change existing ones.

Try It..............

You can conduct your own survey. The Cornell Note-taking system will help you understand the process. Copy the Cornell chart shown below on a sheet of paper. Look for the steps in conducting a survey as you read. After you finish reading, list the steps involved in taking a survey in the Main Points column of your Cornell chart. Write an explanation of each point in the Evidence/Details column.

Main Points	Evidence/Details

Strategy Tip
When you preview the reading, notice that a series of steps is listed. Note these steps in your Cornell chart.

Sample a Survey

You have probably read or heard about the results of a survey. A survey taker asks a number of people what they think about something. Some surveys ask for opinions about a candidate running for office. Some surveys ask questions about a company's new product. Some surveys gather information about the kind of people who live in a community.

People conduct surveys for different reasons. However, all surveys have the same purpose—to collect information.

Many people think that conducting a survey is as easy as asking a bunch of questions. Wrong! A good survey is the result of a series of carefully planned steps. Asking a person a particular question is just one part of the process.

Step 1: Decide on a Topic

Every survey explores a certain topic. To identify the topic, you must think about the reason for the survey. Think about what you will do with the information you collect.

Let's say you're thinking about opening a new ice cream shop in your town. You need to decide how much to charge for each item sold.

Analyzing Data:
Sample a Survey

You need to charge enough to make a profit. You also want the prices to be fair to your customers. A survey could help you set prices. You could conduct a survey to find how much a person in your community is willing to spend for an ice cream cone.

Step 2: Identify the Sample

The people who respond to a survey make up the sample. A sample is a small group that represents the opinions of a much larger group.

It's **unlikely** that you could ask everyone in your town how much an ice cream cone should cost. However, you could survey a small number of those people. You could survey all the high school students or everyone who drives a car.

Would those groups represent all the members of your community? No. People other than students and drivers buy ice cream. Their opinions would not be included in the survey.

A better sample would be every fifth person who leaves the library or every person who attended a school carnival. Those samples would be a broader selection of community members.

Step 3: Decide on the Survey Method

People gather information in three ways. In a mail survey, sample members receive a list of questions in the mail. In a telephone survey, sample members answer questions over the phone. In a personal survey, an interviewer asks the sample members questions in person.

Step 4: Write the Questions

The most important part of conducting a survey is writing the questions. The questions must be clear. They must be easy to understand. They must focus on the topic being explored. Most important, they should not influence the response.

Suppose you ask this question in your ice cream price survey: "Should an ice cream cone cost $1.00 or $1.50?" Does it put a limit on the answer? Yes! A person can respond in only two ways: either $1.00 or $1.50. Maybe the person feels that $1.25 is a fair price. As written, the question does not allow that answer. The person answering the question can't give an honest opinion. A better survey question would be "What do you think is a fair price for an ice cream cone?"

Step 5: Ask the Questions

Now it is time to ask the questions. You've chosen the method of asking questions and contacted the members of the sample. You give them time to respond. Then you collect the responses.

Step 6: Analyze the Data

You count the responses to each survey question. Frequent responses are identified. Sometimes, graphing or charting the results makes them clearer. You think about what you learn from your survey.

The results of the ice cream survey might show that 28 of 50 people said that $1.25 is a fair price for an ice cream cone. Another 17 people said that $1.50 is a fair price. Since those were the top two responses, you might decide to charge $1.35 for a cone.

After you finish reading about surveys, complete your Cornell chart. Then use your notes to write a summary of the selection. The summary should include the important points and details to back them up. Then look over your notes and summary one last time.

Your next step is to conduct a survey of your own. Pick a topic that interests you. Then follow the steps to gather your information. Share your findings with your class.

Apply It. . . . . To check your understanding of the selection, circle the best answer to each question below.

1. What is the purpose of every survey?
   a. to gather information
   b. to analyze information
   c. to identify a topic
   d. to create questions

2. A sample is
   a. the topic of the survey.
   b. a method of questioning.
   c. a small group of people who represent a larger group.
   d. a way of analyzing information.

3. Which of the following is *not* a trait of a good survey question?
   a. easy to understand
   b. focused on the topic being explored
   c. clearly written
   d. influences the response

Test Tip

The selection describes the steps in a process. Question 4 asks about the order of those steps. You probably have the steps in order in your Cornell notes.

4. According to the selection, what should you do immediately before writing the survey questions?
   a. Identify the sample.
   b. Decide on the survey method.
   c. Find a survey topic.
   d. Contact members of the sample group.

5. How might a chart or graph help you analyze survey results?
   a. Looking at a picture is more enjoyable than looking at words.
   b. Data on a chart or a graph is easy to see and comprehend.
   c. Charts and graphs are colorful.
   d. Looking at words can be boring.

Use the lines below to write your answers for numbers 6 and 7. Use your Cornell notes and summary to help you.

6. Name three surveys that you have participated in or heard about. How were they alike? How did they differ?

_____

_____

_____

_____

7. Graph or chart the results of the survey you conducted. If you want to represent your results as a percentage of the whole sample, a pie chart will work well. If you want to show similarities or differences, try a bar graph. If you want to show how something changed over time, choose a line graph. You can use the space below the lines to draw your graph or chart. Then describe how you made your graph or chart.

_____

_____

_____

_____

Computer Design:
Lesson 23 Donna Auguste, American Dreamer

Understand It......

Hint

You can review the KWL Plus strategy on page 12.

This reading profiles a computer designer named Donna Auguste. As an African American female, Donna had to work hard to accomplish her goals. She had to overcome many biases. In this selection, you will read about her life and accomplishments.

Try It..............

The KWL Plus strategy will help you understand the selection. Begin by listing everything you know about computers in the K column. Think about size, weight, what happens when you drop one, how easy or difficult they are to use, what they need to run, and what people do with them. Also consider what you already know about Donna Auguste. The photograph on the next page will give you some information about her.

In the W column, write what you want to know about a career in computer design and about Donna. Keep those questions in mind as you read the selection. Write the answers in the L column. Then use your chart to write a summary of the selection.

Strategy Tip

Consider asking some *how* and *why* questions about the selection.

K (What I know)	W (What I want to know)	L (What I've learned)

Strategy Tip

Do you know what a computer designer does? If you do, include that information in the K column of your chart.

Donna Auguste, American Dreamer

What would your dream computer be like? You might want to take it to class. It would have to fit into your purse or backpack. You'd want it to be lightweight. You wouldn't have room for a keyboard. The computer would have to read your handwriting. Imagine such a computer. Donna Auguste not only imagined it—she also helped design it. It's called the Newton. The Apple Computer Company developed the notebook-sized computer.

Auguste's accomplishment doesn't surprise anyone who knew her as a child. She always had a great curiosity about how things worked. She dismantled doorknobs, doorbells, even toasters. In school, Auguste showed a flair for math and science. She found that some people didn't think a girl could do well in those classes. "Some of the smartest kids in my science class were girls," Auguste recalls, "but those girls did not want to let on that they understood. It was considered a boys' kind of thing."

Life changed for Auguste in the seventh grade. Her class visited a science and technology museum. For the first time, she touched a computer. Before that, she had seen computers only on television.

Computer Design:
Donna Auguste, American Dreamer

No one could explain to Auguste how computers worked. She couldn't find library books about computers, so she visited the museum often.

Auguste persuaded her mother to let her enroll in the only public high school that offered a freshman computer class. It was more than an hour away from the family home in Berkeley, California. "I was fascinated by the manner in which computers make life easier. Whatever you know how to do, computers can help you do it better."

At age 14, Auguste took on a newspaper route. She began saving for college. No one in her family had attended college, but people encouraged her to follow her dream.

Donna Auguste holds her invention, the Newton computer.

Auguste worked hard in high school. Her hard work paid off. She earned high scores on her Scholastic Aptitude Test. The University of California at Berkeley offered her a scholarship. She accepted and began her studies in computer science. Finally, she would learn just how those museum computers worked.

College life wasn't always easy. Auguste ran into **biases** against women. "When professors told students to work in teams, I had a hard time finding partners. Most of the students were males. They'd come right out and say they didn't want to work with a girl."

Auguste never considered giving up on her dreams. She earned a degree in electrical engineering and computer science. She then went to graduate school at Carnegie Mellon University.

Auguste specialized in artificial intelligence in her first job. Her team worked to develop similarities between the way humans think and the way computers work.

Auguste used that experience when she joined Apple Computers. She led a team of 20 computer experts who spent months exploring new ideas for an advanced computer. They wanted their creation to be lightweight and small. They also wanted to build a computer that could be used almost anywhere—even on a busy sidewalk!

The team members settled on what the computer should do. Then they went to work. For two and a half years, group members often worked 18 hour days, seven days a week. Their hard work paid off. The Newton was born.

Vocabulary Tip

Do you know what *biases* means? Read the other words in this paragraph for clues to its meaning.

Apple Computers no longer makes the Newton. However, Auguste's team's **breakthrough** invention led to a number of developments in personal-computer hardware. Some of these new computers are small enough to fit into a shirt pocket.

Today, Auguste is the head of her own company. Freshwater Technologies develops new computer and online technologies. She has three engineering patents from the U.S. Patent and Trademark Office. The Women in Technology International Hall of Fame honored her. Auguste was also featured in the PBS mini-series for children, *Science and the American Dream*. In 1998, she was named one of the 25 most influential women on the World Wide Web.

Now that you have finished reading, go back and complete the L column of your chart. Can you answer every question in the W column? What did you learn about hard work and determination from reading Auguste's story? What did you learn about computer design? The answer is your summary of the reading.

Apply It. . . . . To check your understanding of the reading, circle the best answer to each question below.

1. What trait did Donna Auguste show as a young girl?
   a. dedication
   b. cheerfulness
   c. curiosity
   d. compassion

2. Why did Auguste take on a newspaper route at age 14?
   a. She was saving for a computer.
   b. She was saving for college.
   c. She wanted to buy new clothes.
   d. Her family needed money.

3. What is the Newton?
   a. a college
   b. a museum
   c. a company that makes computers
   d. a notebook-sized computer

4. Why did some classmates refuse to work with Auguste in college?
   a. She was a woman.
   b. Members of her family had not gone to college.
   c. She did not own a computer.
   d. She had poor grades.

5. How did Auguste become interested in computers?
   a. Her mother showed her how to work a computer.
   b. She touched a computer in a museum.
   c. She saw a movie about computers in school.
   d. She read a book that explained how a computer works.

Use the lines below to write your answers for numbers 6 and 7. You can use your KWL chart and summary to help you.

6. Suppose you are giving Auguste the award from the Women in Technology International Hall of Fame. Write a short speech in which you honor her achievements.

_____

_____

_____

_____

7. Suppose you could design a new computer. What would it be able to do? What would it look like? How would it differ from computers currently on the market? What would you name it? Respond to the questions in paragraph form. You can also draw your computer in the space below the lines.

_____

_____

_____

_____

Problem Solving:
Lesson 24 Guess and Check

Understand It......

Hint
You can review the PACA strategy on page 4.

This reading is about a problem-solving method called guess and check. You can use guess and check to figure out word problems in math class. You can also use it in many real-life situations. Use the PACA strategy to help you remember the main points of this selection.

Try It...............

Think about the word *guess* in the title. A guess is a kind of prediction. When you preview the reading, you'll notice a series of steps. They are clues to the selection's main points.

Copy the PACA chart on another sheet of paper. Then make Predictions about the kind of information the selection contains. Think about your predictions as you read. When you're finished reading, you will confirm your predictions.

Strategy Tip
Use your experiences with word problems when making your predictions.

Predictions	Support

Guess and Check

Have you ever entered a contest in which you had to guess how many items were in a container? You might have guessed how many jelly beans are in a glass jug. To win, you needed to make a good guess.

Solving certain kinds of word problems also requires making a good guess. You check your guess. If you are wrong, you make an adjustment. You guess again. Often, you need to make a series of guesses until you find the solution. That problem-solving method is called *guess and check*.

Vocabulary Tip
Most words have more than one meaning. Think about the way *key* is used in this selection. How does the meaning differ from the way *key* is used in the sentence "Josh lost his house key"?

The **key** to using the method well is making good guesses. You base a good guess on known facts. You think about what you need to figure out. You think about what you already know. You use the information to make a good guess. You check your guess. If it is wrong, you make another guess.

You can use guess and check to solve the following problem:

The Hawks soccer team has 15 members. The team played two dozen games last season. Three of the games ended in a tie. The team won twice as many games as it lost. How many games did the Hawks lose last season?

Problem Solving:
Guess and Check

Strategy Tip

Add a prediction about each of these three subheadings to your PACA chart.

Step 1: Identify What You Need to Find
Read the problem again. What are you being asked to find out? The last sentence of the problem contains that information. You must determine the number of games the Hawks lost last season.

Step 2: Identify What You Know
Go back to the problem. Underline the facts given. You need some, but not all, of that information to find a solution. Facts contained in this problem include:

- The team has 15 members.
- The team played 2 dozen, or 24, games last season.
- Three games ended in a tie.
- The team won twice as many games as it lost

Step 3: Use What You Know to Make a Guess
You know the team played 24 games. Three games ended in a tie. That means the total number of games won or lost was 24 − 3, or 21. Use the facts to make a guess.

Perhaps you guess that the team lost 6 games. Check your guess. According to the problem, the team won twice as many games as it lost. According to your guess, the team won 12 games and lost 6. Does 12 + 6 equal 21, which is the total number of games won or lost? No. Therefore, you must guess again.

Try a higher number, such as 7. That means the team won 14 games and lost 7. Does 14 + 7 equal 21? Yes! Therefore, the solution is 7.

As you can see, this problem-solving method involves much more than random guessing. When you use guess and check, you perform a series of steps. Each step leads you closer to a solution. The next time you need to solve a math word problem, try using the guess-and-check method.

Now that you have finished reading about guess and check, look at your PACA chart. Put check marks next to the predictions that you confirmed. Then revise or add to your predictions. Note important points that you had not thought of. Add them to your list of predictions. Finally, add support for each prediction.

Apply It. . . . . To check your understanding of the selection, circle the best answer to each question below.

1. What is guess and check?
   a. a math game
   b. a contest
   c. a math problem
   d. a problem-solving method

2. According to the selection, what should you do after reading the problem?
   a. List what you know.
   b. Write the problem on a sheet of paper.
   c. Identify what you need to find out.
   d. Make a guess.

3. A good guess is
   a. based on facts.
   b. made quickly.
   c. a guess that is correct.
   d. a guess that everybody agrees on.

4. What is the author's purpose for writing this selection?
   a. to show that math is fun
   b. to teach a process
   c. to entertain others
   d. to convince students that math is important

5. What is the tone of the selection?
   a. humorous
   b. formal
   c. informative
   d. sad

Use the lines below to write your answers for numbers 6 and 7. Use your PACA notes to help you.

6. Al is six years older than Joe. Their combined ages equal 34. Explain how you could use guess and check to figure out Al's age.

_____

_____

_____

7. How are the guess-and-check method and the PACA strategy similar?

_____

_____

_____

Unit 5 Review
Reading in Mathematics

*I*n this unit, you have practiced using the KWL Plus, Cornell Note-taking, PACA, and Concept Building reading strategies. Choose one strategy, and use it when you read the selection below. Use a separate sheet of paper to draw charts, take notes, and summarize what you learn.

Hint *Remember that all reading strategies have activities for before, during, and after reading. To review these steps, look back at Unit 1 or at the last page of this book.*

Figuring Miles Per Gallon

On every new car is a sticker that explains how many miles the car gets to a gallon of gas. That number is called the car's *mileage*. The more miles to a gallon of gas the car gets, the less the car costs to run.

Suppose you are buying a used car that gets only 6 miles to the gallon. You will spend a lot of money on gas.

You can easily check the miles per gallon that your car gets. First, though, you need to know some terms. One of these is **mpg**. That stands for *miles per gallon*. Another term is **odometer**. That is the equipment on the car's dashboard that shows how many miles you have driven the car.

To calculate mpg, use these steps:

Step 1 When you stop for gas, fill the tank up completely. Write down the reading on the odometer.

Step 2 The next time you buy gas again, fill the tank completely. Then write down the odometer reading. Also write down the number of gallons you needed to fill the tank.

Step 3 Find out how many miles you drove from the first odometer reading to the second. Subtract your old odometer reading from your new odometer reading.

Step 4 Divide the number of miles you drove by the number of gallons of gas needed to fill your tank. That number of miles is your mpg.

Here is the formula:

Mpg = new odometer reading – old odometer reading ÷ gallons of gas needed to fill the tank

Let's say you filled your tank in one city. Your odometer read 3,876. You travel to another city. Your odometer now reads 4,071. You fill your tank with 13 gallons of gas. To figure out how many miles you are getting to a gallon, you would do the following calculations:

1. Find out how many miles you traveled by subtracting the first odometer reading from the second.

$$4071 - 3876 = 195$$

You have traveled 195 miles.

2. Divide 195 by the number of gallons of gas you used. That number is 13.

195 ÷ 13 = 15

Your car gets 15 miles to a gallon of gas, or 15 mpg.

The formula looks like this:

(4071 − 3876) ÷ 13 =
195 ÷ 13 = 15

Knowing how to find mpg is a useful skill. It can tell you exactly how much your car costs to run.

Use your notes and charts to help you answer the questions below.

1. What is an odometer?
   a. a device that determines miles per gallon
   b. the way you calculate miles per gallon
   c. a device that shows how many miles you have driven
   d. the number of miles you have driven a car

2. Knowing your mpg can be useful if
   a. you want to know how fast you are going.
   b. you want to know how much gas you have left.
   c. you want to know how expensive your car is to run.
   d. you want to see if your car is too expensive to buy.

3. To calculate mpg, after you know how many miles you have driven since you last filled your gas tank, you first
   a. subtract the number of miles you have driven from the first odometer reading.
   b. convert to mpg.
   c. divide that number by the number of miles you have traveled to find mpg.
   d. divide that number by the number of gallons of gas you used.

4. Suppose your odometer reads 7544 miles when you fill your car with gas. The next time you fill your gas tank your odometer reads 7765. Your tank takes 13 gallons of gas. How many miles per gallon (mpg) does your car get?

_____

_____

5. Suppose you are selling your car and it has an mpg reading of 27. Explain to a buyer why this is important.

_____

_____

Vocabulary Handbook

Everyone puzzles over some words when they read. People approach unknown words in different ways. You may look up a word you do not know. Someone else may look for how a word is used in a sentence. In this handbook, you will learn some new methods of figuring out the meaning of new words. You may also review methods you already know.

Using Word Maps to Understand Unknown Words

You may know right away that you need to understand a new word. One method of figuring out the meaning of the word is to make a word map. When you use a word map, you collect words in the selection that can help you understand the meaning of the new word.

Suppose you are reading an article called "Understanding the Nucleus." You know that you need to understand the word *nucleus* to understand the reading. First, preview the reading to find information about the word. Here is how a word map about the word *nucleus* might look:

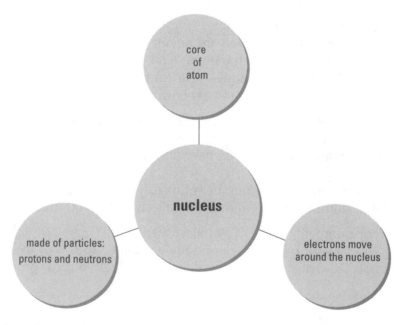

The reader who made this word map now knows that a nucleus is the core of an atom, that its core is made of protons and neutrons, and that electrons move around the nucleus. Now he or she can understand the selection better.

In these exercises, you will learn more methods of figuring out the meanings of the words you read.

Exercise 1   Words with Multiple Meanings

Understand It...... A word may appear in different subject areas and have a different meaning in each one. Here are two ways to help you understand words with multiple, or several, meanings.

- **Choose from among the meanings you know.** You may know that the word *cell* can mean two things. A *cell* can be a basic unit of living matter. A *cell* can also be a small room in a prison. When you see a word that you know has more than one meaning, think about what you are reading. Which meaning would fit better in the subject you are reading about?

- **Pause if the word you know doesn't make sense.** For example, you may know one meaning of the word *legend*. A *legend* can be a story that is handed down through the years by a people. But read this sentence:

> Look at the map **legend** to find the symbol for camping spots.

The meaning in that sentence is different from the one you may know. If you find a word you think you know, but that word doesn't make sense, look it up. That word probably has multiple meanings.

Below are two passages that use the same words in different ways. Read both passages. Then look at the words in bold type. Use the suggestions above to understand what the words mean in each passage.

> **Example 1**
> I wanted to make a circle graph. I wanted to show the different amounts of fruits the country imports. I divided the circle into six **sectors**. Each sector showed how much of one fruit the country imported. The sector for apples was the largest. The country imports more apples than any other fruit. I plan to make graphs now whenever I can. It takes some **intelligence** to make them, but it is worth it.
>
> **Example 2**
> They were the fly boys. According to one officer, these war pilots were not shy.
>
> "Once, they had orders to fly to a new **sector**." No one had flown there before. The flyers wouldn't do it until they had better **intelligence**," the officer said.

Try It.............. To check your understanding of the vocabulary words, circle the best answer to each question below.

1. In Example 1, the word *sectors* means
   a. parts.
   b. angles.
   c. circles.
   d. lines.

Words with Multiple Meanings

2. Which of these is the best word for *intelligence* in Example 2?
   a. information
   b. success
   c. understanding
   d. mental ability

3. Which of the following statements is *false*?
   a. In Example 1, *sector* is another word for "section."
   b. The meaning of *intelligence* is the same in both examples.
   c. In Example 2, *sector* means a "specific area."
   d. In Example 1, *intelligence* means "mental ability."

More words with multiple meanings: Sometimes words that we use every day have different meanings in different content areas. Read the two definitions for each word below. Then choose a word from the list that fits both definitions. Write the word on the line.

date	bed	bark	yard	cape

4. _____

   Common use: a sleeveless garment worn around the shoulders
   Geography: a piece of land extending into the water

5. _____

   Common use: the fruit of one type of palm tree
   History: the exact point in time at which an event takes place

6. _____

   Common use: the ground around or next to a house or other building
   Mathematics: a measure of length

7. _____

   Common use: the short, sharp noise made by dogs
   Science: the outer covering of a tree

8. _____

   Common use: a piece of furniture on which to sleep
   Geography: the bottom of a river

Exercise 2 Context Clues: Part I

Understand It...... One of the ways active readers figure out the meaning of words they do not know is by using context clues. They can help you understand what a word means.

- **Look at the words around the word you do not know.** These words can help you define the new word.

- **Look for all the times the word is used.** Sometimes a word you don't know is repeated or restated. Look at the places the word is used for clues.

Read the paragraph. Use context clues to understand the words in bold type.

> Food chains are chains of living things that depend on each other. **Herbivores** are animals that eat plants. A bird that eats seeds is an example of a **herbivore**. Meat-eaters, or **carnivores**, are at the top of the food chain. A wolf is one example of a **carnivore**. **Carnivores** eat **herbivores**. Some **carnivores** eat other **carnivores**, too.

Try It.............. To check your understanding of the vocabulary entries, circle the best answer to each question below.

1. What is the best description of *carnivore*?
   a. a plant-eating animal
   b. an animal-eating animal
   c. a herbivore
   d. an animal eaten by bacteria and fungi

2. Which of these statements is correct?
   a. A herbivore is a plant that gets its food from the sun.
   b. A herbivore is an animal that eats only animals.
   c. A herbivore is an animal that eats plants and animals.
   d. A herbivore is an animal that eats only plants.

Use context clues to figure out the meaning of the term in bold type. Write a definition for that term in the space provided.

3. While sales at the Lakeland Corporation have nearly tripled, sales at the Regis Corporation are **plummeting**.

   _____

   _____

4. The contract negotiations are becoming increasingly **partisan**; neither management nor the labor union is willing to give in.

   _____

   _____

Exercise 3   Context Clues: Part II

Understand It...... Sometimes writers make it easy for readers to understand difficult words. They add definitions, restatements, or synonyms. Other times authors use examples that show the word's meaning, or compare or contrast the word to other known words. Once you know these tools, you may find yourself understanding more of what you read. Here are some of those tools:

- **Definitions, restatements, and synonyms.** If authors think a word may be difficult, often they will help their readers by defining the word right there. They may also restate the meaning of the word or show the meaning through a synonym. Here is an example of each:

> *Definition:* She studied **biology**, which is the study of living things.
>
> *Restatement:* The **goslings**, those fuzzy baby geese, waddled after their mother.
>
> *Synonym:* Dan was feeling so **distressed**, so upset, by the grade he got, that he refused to come to the party.

- **Meaning through example.** Sometimes authors use an example to show the meaning of a word in action. Examples may be shown by words such as *for instance, for example,* and *such as.* The following sentence shows you how it works:

> The scientist found many basic **raw materials,** such as minerals, while in the field collecting samples.

- **Comparisons and contrasts.** A sentence may include a comparison that shows how the unknown word is like another word. The words *like, as,* and *similar to* may signal this. A contrast shows how a word is unlike another word. Look for words such as *but, however, instead, on the contrary,* and *on the other hand* in contrasts. For example:

> *Comparison:* Carol was **as** congenial as the friendliest person I know.
>
> *Contrast:* Little Danny was **sorrowful,** but his new toy made him happy.

Try It.............. Read the following sentences.

> Production at the Dallas division of the Lakeland Corporation is completely **automated.** However, production at the Columbus division is done by hand.

1. Which words act as a signal and help you figure out the meaning of the word *automated?*

_____

2. What does the word *automated* mean?

_____

Read the paragraphs below. Use context tools to help you understand the meaning of the words in bold type. Then answer the questions below.

Impeachment is a charge against a high official for a crime. It is not common in the United States. President Andrew Johnson was **impeached** after the Civil War. The Senate held a trial. Johnson had **vetoed** many bills instead of signing them as laws. He and Congress fought. Johnson wanted to make it easier for Southern states to rejoin the country, but Congress did not.

Finally, the Senate held the trial. Although each side offered evidence, Johnson was not convicted. Instead, he was **acquitted** of the charges against him. He served out his term in office.

To check your understanding of the vocabulary entries, circle the best answer to each question below.

3. Impeachment is
   a. a trial during which a high official is tried.
   b. a charge against a high official.
   c. the conviction of an official for high crimes.
   d. the process of trying a high official for a crime.

4. Which is the best definition for the word *veto?*
   a. to sign a bill into law.
   b. to vote for a law.
   c. to argue against a bill that will be made into a law.
   d. to reject a bill and not allow it to become a law.

5. If you are *acquitted* of a crime, you
   a. are not convicted.
   b. must go to trial.
   c. can not be convicted of a crime.
   d. are convicted.

Exercise 4   Signal Words

Understand It...... You often see words in directions. They tell you in what order to do things and allow you to follow a reading selection more easily. Here are some of those words:

- **Words that give you steps.** You may often see these words when you are reading a science experiment. You will see them in writing that describes a process. You also will see them when you are following directions. If you put together a bike, for example, you may see a series of steps that you should take.

Some of these words are number words, such as *first*, *second*, and *last*. Others help you keep track of the order in which you should do something, such as *before* and *then*. Here is an example of how you might see these words:

> **First,** put the sugar and the water in the pan. **Second,** turn up the heat to high. **Next,** cook until the mixture bubbles. **Finally,** let it cool.

- **Words that tell you what is coming next.** Often writers will tell you what is coming next by using these signal words. You may remember seeing words such as *therefore* or *in conclusion*. These words will give you clues to what the writer is doing. Notice the signal words in the sentences below.

> Let me **restate** this point. No one is sure what this drug will do. **Therefore,** I will not approve it. **In conclusion,** I must say that no one should ever take this unsafe drug.

When you see the words *in conclusion*, you know the writer is signaling that he or she is reviewing, or summing up, the selection.

Read the paragraphs below. Use signal words to help you understand how the words in bold type are used. Then answer the questions below.

> If you plan to do this experiment, follow these steps. **First,** gather all of your materials. **Second,** clean your equipment well. **Last,** make sure all of your equipment is working. If you do all these things in this order, you will have done all you can to make sure your experiment will work.
>
> **In conclusion,** let me end my paper by summarizing for you the most important conclusions of my research. **First,** there is not enough information available to say if the horned bat will ever return. Even

though we have an idea that the bat has found other places to live, we do not know that for certain. **Second**, there are no plans to create a new habitat near here. **Finally**, and **most important**, there is no money to continue studying this topic. I am afraid the horned bats have to survive on their own.

Try It. . . . . To check your understanding of the signal words, circle the best answer to each question below.

1. Which of these steps comes last?
   a. preparing for the experiment
   b. making sure the equipment is working
   c. cleaning the equipment well
   d. getting together all materials

2. What is the author signaling when she writes *in conclusion*?
   a. that she is briefly reviewing her findings
   b. that she is at the beginning of her arguments
   c. that this is the research that took the most time
   d. that these are the steps that listeners should follow

3. What is the *most important* conclusion of the scientist writing the second paragraph?
   a. Horned bats are extinct.
   b. There is no money left for research on the bats.
   c. No one can say if the horned bats will return.
   d. There are no new habitats for the horned bats.

4. Read the following list. Number the entries in time order.
   _____ Second, listen for a dial tone.
   _____ Finally, tell the dispatcher where the fire is.
   _____ First, pick up the phone.
   _____ After that, dial 911.

5. Number the following sentences in correct order.
   _____ First, I missed the bus that I take to school.
   _____ My first day of school was very hectic.
   _____ Luckily, I found a seat in the back of class, so no one saw me come in late.
   _____ As a result, I was 15 minutes late.
   _____ Then I had to wait ten extra minutes so my mom could drive me.

Exercise 5   Prefixes and Suffixes

Understand It...... Prefixes are word parts that are added to the beginnings of words. Suffixes are word parts that are added to the end of words. These add-ons change the meaning of a word. You may already know more of these than you think. Test yourself using the following chart.

Prefixes	Meanings	Examples
non-, in-, im-, il-, ir-, un-	*not*	*Nonverbal* means "not verbal." *Insecure* means "not secure." *Unselfish* means "not selfish."
de-, dis-	*away from* or *the opposite of*	*Dislike* means "the opposite of like."
re-	*again*	*Redo* means "to do again."
pre-, fore-	*before* or *ahead of time*	*Preview* means "to see before."
trans-	*across* or *to the other side of*	*Transfer* means "to move something from one person or thing to another person or thing."

Suffixes	Meanings	Examples
-less	*without*	*Meaningless* means "without meaning."
-ful, -ous	*full of*	*Thankful* means "full of thanks."
-er, -or, -ist	*someone or thing that does something*	A *conformist* is a "person who conforms."
-able, -ible	*can* or *able to be*	*Adjustable* means "able to be adjusted."
-ship, -ment, -ness, -hood	*the state of* or *the condition of*	*Personhood* means "the state of being a person."

Try It.............. Read the sentences below. Decide on the meaning of the words by looking at their prefixes and suffixes.

1. The root word in *discontinue* is: _____

2. *Discontinue* means _____

3. The root word in *beautiful* is: _____

4. *Beautiful* means _____

5. The root word in *unacceptable* is: _____

6. Unacceptable means _____